THE DAY I DIED

Finding Hope in Suffering

by Melanie Pritchard

May this book enrich your faith!

Blessings,
Melanie Pritchard

Cover and interior design by T. Schluenderfritz

Cover Photo by Carlos Weaver

Printed in the United States of America

ISBN: 978-0-615-49488-3

Dedication

*To my Lord and Savior for showing me
your great power and mercy!*

*To my husband, Doug, you are my greatest love
and strongest example of what it means to be holy.
Thank you for standing by me "in sickness and in
health." Our family life is heaven on earth!*

*To my children Brady and Gabriella, you are unrepeatable,
irreplaceable and unique. The day you were born the world
changed for the better because you are in it. There never was
or ever will be anyone like you—because you are SPECIAL!*

*To my entire family and dear friends, your love for me gave
me the strength to survive. I could not have done it without
your constant support and care. I love you with all my heart!*

*To every doctor, nurse, tech, blood donor, and all who
were involved in my care, thank you for not giving up
on Gabriella and me, and fighting for our survival.
I am eternally grateful to each one of you!*

*To all those who prayed for me, I am overwhelmed
by your generosity and pleased to tell you that your
prayers worked! Gabriella and I are alive and well!*

Acknowledgements

Thank you to my family and friends for writing your accounts and helping me piece together the great miracle that took place.

Thank you, Patrick Madrid, Mark Hart, Jason Evert, Gail Pritchard, Sherry Welsch, Brooke Burns, Maryrose Lins, Jane Cavolina, Ted Schluenderfritz, Mary Moore, Mike and Sharon Phelan, and Bonnie Tyminski for your invaluable help during the writing process.

Thank you, Carlos Weaver and Ane Marie Quigley for sharing your talents.

Thank you to all who shared your suffering with me; your words inspired me as I was writing this book.

Contents

FOREWORD

I did not know who Melanie Pritchard was when I first read in an urgent message about her on Facebook. It said that she was a young Catholic mom in grave danger of dying as a result of complications during childbirth.

"What?" I asked myself. "How often does *that* happen anymore? Hers must be a really unusual case." And so it was.

Like countless others on Facebook and Twitter that day, I alerted my friends about Melanie's plight, asking them to join me in praying for her. At first, I wasn't even sure if the baby she was giving birth to had made it through alive. But gradually, as this life-and-death drama unfolded, we received updates that not only had her tiny cherub Gabriella survived the delivery in good health, but that Melanie herself had also pulled through an unbelievably close call and was likely to survive, heal, and go home to be with husband Doug, son Brady, and newborn Gabriella.

My calling Melanie's harrowing medical ordeal a "close call" is truly a bona-fide understatement. As you will discover in this book, she quite literally passed through the valley of the shadow of death. She traversed down a deep and dark path into that valley, one out of which few women return. And her family! Melanie's family and friends lived through interminable hours of anguish, convinced that what little flicker of life Melanie still had left in her would be extinguished suddenly and without warning, and she would be gone.

The odds against Melanie's survival were formidable. She endured blood poisoning from amniotic fluid, heart failure, catastrophic hemorrhaging, and three back-to-back emergency major surgeries — *plus* she was clinically dead for upwards of 10 minutes as the trauma team fought frantically to resuscitate Melanie. That combination of biomedical catastrophes would be enough to vanquish anyone. But our good God did not permit this young mother to remain in the valley of the shadow of death.

Through the prayers and tears of her family and friends, as well as those of countless others who, like I, did not know Melanie personally, a great outpouring of prayer and supplication rose up to heaven on her behalf. Those who rallied prayerfully to her defense simply asked the Lord to save her life and restore her to health, if it be His will.

God's will surely is mysterious, and we sometimes do not receive the answer to our prayers that we expect and long for. Not so in this case. Against all odds, as her doctors and nurses grimly warned, Melanie's miraculous survival and recovery was clearly God's will. It was the occasion for a shining example of both the power of prayer and of the Body of Christ in action; the prayerful, petitioning concern on the part of the many for the sake of the one.

As St. Paul reminds us in 2 Corinthians 12:12, 26-28:

> For just as the body is one and has many members, and all the members of the body, though many, are one body, so it is with Christ. . . . If one member suffers, all suffer together; if one member is honored, all rejoice together. Now you are the body of Christ and individually members of it.

Perhaps the deepest, most important lesson to be learned from this story is not that God works miracles (He does). Nor is it that prayer changes things (it does). Nor is it even that, sometimes, according to God's mysterious, loving providence, bad things do happen to good people — for, as we all know from painful experience, that surely does happen.

No, I believe that the really *fundamental* lesson to be learned from Melanie's terrifying ordeal is that of . . . trust. Trusting in God. Trusting that regardless of whatever crosses He may deign to grace us with, He will also keep His promise to give rest to the weary and heavily burdened.

Reading this book, I am reminded of the gloriously simple yet battlefield-powerful phrase which Christ taught St. Faustina to pray: "Jesus, I trust in you."

Trust. That is the deeper lesson to be learned here. It's a lesson that reverberated through Melanie, her husband, her family and friends, and throughout the Body of Christ. It burst forth through Catholic radio, across parishes, and into convents, rectories, seminaries, and schools; it lit up Facebook, Twitter, and everywhere else that the grace of God penetrated with the promise of hope. And it found its way to people like me, those who had never heard of Melanie before then.

Well, there's nothing more to tell you except for this: As you read this book, I hope you will pause, here and there, and with all your heart whisper that prayer: "Jesus, I trust in you." My own prayer for you, dear reader, is that this story will help you to always trust Him without hesitation or reserve. May God bless you.

— PATRICK MADRID (www.patrickmadrid.com) is the publisher of *Envoy* Magazine, author of *Search and Rescue,* and editor of the *Surprised by Truth* series.

INTRODUCTION

When I woke up from death to find myself being called "a miracle," I searched my mind for insight into what my friends and family were telling me, only to find that my memories were absent...gone. I was in a hospital bed, unable to recall the incredible trauma that nearly took my life and the life of my daughter, and had to rely solely on everyone else's account. I felt the physical pain of it all, but had no idea why I was in pain or why breathing was so hard.

Confused, I began asking questions, trying to figure it all out. For every question I asked family members and friends, tears of great pain rolled down their faces as they did their best to recap the event surrounding the birth of my second child. As the people who were closest to me shared their deepest, most heart-wrenching accounts, I listened without emotion. It seemed like I was hearing an incredible story about some other woman. Even though they were telling me my own story, I felt like an outsider looking in, trying to absorb every piece of information and drive it into my memory. A part of me wanted to feel the pain of what everyone else was going through because they all had these feelings I did not have.

What you are about to read is a story handed down to me from my family and friends detailing their love, friendship, and affection for me as wife, mother, sister, daughter, and friend. This book revolves around the day my heart stopped beating, but is unpacked for you as each person tells his or her side of the story, interwoven with glimpses into my relationships with those who shared. Each story was a piece of the puzzle I longed to complete in my own mind. I will never know this story from my own perspective, but this book has helped me to experience the day that changed my life forever. Through pain and tears, my family and friends relived the worst and best day of their lives to share their accounts with me. I invite you on a journey with me to uncover why my survival has been called miraculous.

I have many reasons to capture and reflect upon this incident in my life, but more than anything, I hope to reveal the great power of prayer, and the way God works through tragedy and suffering to provide hope and healing. I have written this book for my daughter, Gabriella (Ella, as we call her), to offer her an account of the day of her birth. The book is for me, too, so I can know the miracles that transpired on that day. It is also for people who have suffered a loss—whether it is the loss of a family member or friend, health, identity, or loss of the will to live and move forward. I hope my story reveals the strength that comes from people who reach out and sacrifice to serve those who need them.

Chapter One
A LITTLE BACKGROUND

*P*eople who know me would say I am strong, a bit
feisty, a fighter, and a defender of justice. I am a
faithful practicing Catholic. By trade I am a speaker, and
consider myself a modern-day disciple fighting for souls
to get them to heaven. But, on July 28, 2010, it was my
life that would need fighting for, as a battle was on for my
soul. My daily prayer is "Lord, do with me as you will today
for your greater glory." He answers that prayer regularly
by sending people into my life that need help and healing
or by calling on me to do things big and small. I willingly
open myself up to God's calling, and I do so knowing I may
have to suffer, as God's plan doesn't always look pretty, and
knowing he permits bad things to happen so we may serve
his greater good.

Acquainted With Evil

I saw the devil's fingerprints when I witnessed an
abortion on the TV in my seventh grade classroom during a
showing of *The Silent Scream*, produced in 1984 by former
abortion doctor Bernard Nathanson. Even at that age, I
saw the face of evil in this destructive act. After watching
the video, I was empowered to fight for life, squash evil,
and learn as much as I could in order to convince others
to do the same. Fighting for the lives of the unborn, of

the helpless, and of those silenced, I became loud. I knew my voice had to speak for those who could not speak for themselves. My greatest desire and mission in life was to end abortion, and as I uncovered the lies surrounding this great evil, I began to develop programs and give talks about how to do so.

The Ups and Downs

Gathering, researching, reflecting, writing, and becoming a self-taught expert on the subject of abortion landed me a job as the Education Director for Life Educational Corporation. There, I provided for most of the educational needs of Arizona Right to Life for four years. During this time, I was the chair of the annual statewide Arizona March and Rally for Life, where thousands gathered to unite for life. I spoke locally and nationally, educating many to see into the lies of the culture of death, and even founded my own pro-life, pro-love, pro-family organization called the Foundation for Life and Love.

The role of a pro-life speaker has its ups and downs. The upside is knowing my work is saving lives and protecting women from making the worst decision of their lives. The downside is that I am always on the devil's radar. If God is the source of all life, then the devil is surely against life. As a pro-life advocate, I have to spiritually protect myself, my family, and all those I work with through prayer. I am often in the midst of a battle between good and evil. The evil can be strong and defiant, but never have I feared it, as I always cover myself with the Lord. Only fools would enter this line of work on their own. Only with the strength of God working through and around me can I do this type of ministry. Many times I have felt attacked by the evil one, but I am constantly vigilant in knowing where my enemy is at all times.

My Prayer

Almost every time I set out to do my pro-life work, I opened my Bible to Ephesians 6 and read verses 10–20. The words gave me spiritual protection from whatever might be trying to harm me or the people I was with.

> Finally, draw your strength from the Lord and from his mighty power. Put on the armor of God so that you may be able to stand firm against the tactics of the devil. For our struggle is not with flesh and blood but with the principalities, with the powers, with the world rulers of this present darkness, with the evil spirits in the heavens. Therefore, put on the armor of God, that you may be able to resist on the evil day and, having done everything, to hold your ground. So stand fast with your loins girded in truth, clothed with righteousness as a breastplate, and your feet shod in readiness for the gospel of peace. In all circumstances, hold faith as a shield, to quench all flaming arrows of the evil one. And take the helmet of salvation and the sword of the Spirit, which is the word of God. With all prayer and supplication, pray at every opportunity in the Spirit. To that end, be watchful with all perseverance and supplication for all the holy ones and also for me, that speech may be given me to open my mouth, to make known with boldness the mystery of the gospel for which I am an ambassador in chains, so that I may have the courage to speak as I must.[1]

No Accident

On July 28, 2010, a battle for my soul occurred in the place where I have defended others for so many years; this time, the attack was on my womb. "The flaming arrow" was aimed at my motherhood and my unborn child. The devil's "tactic" was to take me out not once, but four times! God, with his "mighty power," released the "sword of the spirit" and placed the right people in the right places to save my life. Furthermore, many from around the world "held their ground," calling upon the Lord, and "praying at every opportunity" which sent the "armor of God" to be my shield. Many people find themselves in a hospital because of an accident, but this was no accident. All I can call it is the incident. The incident changed my life and made living, breathing, walking miracles out of my newborn child and me. And now, the Lord has opened the airways of my lungs so that "speech may be given to me to open my mouth, to make known with boldness the mystery of the gospel for which I am an ambassador in chains, so that I may have the courage to speak as I must." How the words of Ephesians mean more to me now than they ever did before!

When I woke up from the biggest fight of my life and my family informed me of what happened, I was not angry. I was strangely enough at peace. When the words came out of their mouths recapping my sudden death and survival, I knew that God had permitted this to happen to me for a greater good.

Chapter Two
Marriage and Babies

*M*y favorite day is St. Patrick's Day. I have fond memories of making donuts with my Grandma Welsch, decked out in green attire from head to toe while singing and dancing to Irish songs. As a child, I dreamed of getting married on St. Patrick's Day.

Meeting Doug

The year 2006 was a very busy one for me. I was teaching part time at the community college, running Refuge Clothing (my t-shirt company), and traveling and speaking about chastity and life issues in between. When I finally made the decision to follow God's plan for my life versus my own, my life became more exciting than I could have ever imagined. I traveled to places I had once dreamed of seeing and met some of the most incredible people. Marriage was a distant thought in my mind; I was not worried about whether I was supposed to get married or remain single, and I was trying to live in the present. Yes, there were guys who asked me out here and there, but no one I thought had marriage potential. I must admit, I was so content and at peace with my life that the thought of dating seemed like it might ruin the good thing I had going. My openness to dating was a half-opened door I was ready to slam shut at any moment—that is, until I met Doug.

He was new in town, and knew some of my friends. We were both at an event where I was speaking to a group of teenagers, and he was there to see his friend Kemi play in the band. There was something different about Doug than most guys I had met. He was kind, strong, confident, and made faith his first priority.

We dated for nine months. Around the seventh month, we were taking a ride and talking about how we envisioned getting married, if that was where God was leading this relationship. Doug, who is also Irish to the core with his black hair and fair skin, said, "I think it would be cool to get married on St. Patrick's Day." My eyes widened, and with uncontrollable excitement I said, "That has always been my dream." Then we both said at the same time, "St. Patty's Day is on a Saturday next year!" We both smiled, realizing that the other had already looked on a calendar for possible marriage dates although we were not even engaged yet. A month later, Doug knelt down on one knee and proposed to me. I said, "Yes!!" Eight months later, March 17, 2007, we married on our favorite day of the year.

The Way He Looks at Me

People always ask me, "What is it about Doug that made you want to marry him?" First of all, when we were dating, I prayed a lot and the Lord confirmed over and over to me that I should continue in this relationship. So I did. One of the things that attracted me to Doug was our mutual affection for reading. In the later months of dating, Doug regularly read books about St. Joseph. One day I asked him, "Why do you read so much about St. Joseph?" Without skipping a beat and with complete sincerity in his voice he replied, "St. Joseph knew how to love a woman perfectly [Mary], and I think you deserve to be loved perfectly, so I am trying to learn how." My heart melted to mush. No one had ever said something like that to me before. I thought, "I could marry a man who wants to love me perfectly!"

Whenever I am with couples, I pay attention to how they look at one another. I can tell a lot about a couple's relationship from that. My grandfather Philip used to look at my grandma Doris with the most loving eyes; he so adored her. My Aunt Mary Lou and Uncle Bob were high school sweethearts and have been married for 47 years. He still looks at her with a glow in his eyes, and when she says something funny, he still laughs so hard, finding her entertaining after all those years. It is the cutest thing to watch. I wanted my husband to look at me like my grandfather looked at my grandma and my uncle at my aunt. After dating Doug a while and seeing that same look in his eyes, I knew he was the one I wanted by my side forever. The love he has in his eyes is so strong that sometimes I have to look away because it is too much for me!

Beginning Our Life Together

On St. Patrick's Day 2007, Doug wore green socks under his wedding attire and I wore green shoes under mine. The Mass was beautiful, and after, we enjoyed great food and our wonderful friends while we danced the night away at the reception. Then we headed off to Maui for our honeymoon, where we fell more and more in love with one another. A few weeks later we found out that I was pregnant. Honeymoon baby!

We were so excited, but I am not going to lie, fear also entered my heart as I realized I was going to be a mother and it would no longer just be Doug and me. For 29 years I had come and gone as I pleased and had nothing holding me back from anything. Now, within a month's time, I was married and with child. Life was changing fast. I knew deep down having a child was something I wanted, but at the same time, I realized I would be responsible for this child for at least 18 years—a long time!

Nine months went by as my belly grew and grew and on December 9, 2007, Brady Douglas Pritchard arrived. I was head over heels in love! Never did I know I could love someone so much. Instead of thinking, "I have to take care of this child for 18 years," I started thinking, sadly, "I only have 18 years with him before he goes off to college. That is too short. I want more time!" My heart melted with every look, every coo, every kiss, and every hug.

The adventure and excitement I used to have in my single life could not compare to my family life with Doug and Brady. It was so fulfilling! Since we wanted a big family, after a year, we decided to try to get pregnant with our second child. Month by month went by and our frustration grew because we were not getting pregnant. We could not understand how it was so easy on our honeymoon, and now it was so difficult. We saw our obstetrician and he said that if a year passed and we were not pregnant, he would begin testing.

Chapter Three
A Year Passed and No Baby

A year went by and my sadness grew each month that I was not pregnant. I prayed a lot and tried so hard to trust, but it was difficult. My OB/GYN prescribed fertility-enhancing drugs, which I took for a few months with no success. He also tested my follicle stimulating hormone (FSH) levels and shared that they were in normal range. Then I found out about a test called hysterosalpingogram (HSG), an x-ray that uses a dye contrast to view the inside of the uterus and fallopian tubes to see if there is a blockage. I was interested in having it done, so I went to see a fertility specialist a friend recommended. I was skeptical about going to see a doctor of this sort; I was uncertain about his Catholic moral caliber. The pro-life side of me was intrigued to see a fertility clinic firsthand. I warned Doug the moment we entered the doctor's office: "Be very wary of what the specialist tells us because he might try to sell us on fertility practices contrary to our beliefs."

The Disappointed Doctor

At our initial appointment, the fertility specialist sat down with us and looked at all the test results my regular OB/GYN gave me; he seemed concerned. He told me my FSH levels were too high for a woman my age (32 at the time). I told him that my OB/GYN had told me they were normal. He said that he didn't agree, and that I would never get pregnant without this fertility clinic's "help." In his words, we needed to "act fast if we wanted to get pregnant." Then he insisted we immediately try procedures like in vitro fertilization (IVF) and artificial insemination. We declined both.

Then with great disappointment in his demeanor and for his failed attempt to sell us the most expensive procedures, I said, "Doctor, we trust in God, and even though these tests indicate that I may have trouble getting pregnant, you do not know my God. My God is bigger than these tests." His eyes widened at my response. I continued, "If God only blesses us with one child, then we are okay with that. The only reason we're here is to see if anything is wrong. All we want from you is an HSG procedure. That will at least help us determine if there are any problems with my fallopian tubes and uterus." He reluctantly agreed to do it.

The HSG Test

I returned a few days later for the procedure. When it was completed, he told me everything looked fine; there was no blockage. Then, he mentioned that the procedure itself makes women more fertile for three months. That statement brought me hope, but also made me question this doctor's ethics, since I was the one who suggested it. If this could increase my fertility, then why not mention it before the more invasive procedures? Was he even interested in helping us or was he just out to make a dollar?

I will never forget hearing the doctor telling me I would probably never get pregnant on my own. I gave a talk around this time, and I opened up to the audience about my difficulty in getting pregnant. I said, "God is enough for me. He would still be enough for me even if I had nothing and no one in my life. God blessed me with the gift of Doug and if it were just Doug and me for life, then that would be enough too. But God blessed us with the gift of Brady, and if that is all God blesses us with, then that is sufficient for us. God alone was enough in the first place." Although the doctor was correct about the increase in my fertility after the HSG procedure, he was completely wrong about my ability to become pregnant. Three days later, I was pregnant!

Is It a Boy or a Girl?

Becoming pregnant was heaven sent. Doug and I were excited, relieved, and grateful to have another life growing inside of me. During this time, my brother, Larry, and sister-in-law, Remi, were also trying to get pregnant. When we revealed the good news to the family, we found out Larry and Remi had their own bit of good news. They were pregnant, too. We did all the calculations and Remi and I were due on the exact same date! The family was ecstatic!

I would have been happy with either a brother or a sister for Brady. But, I was eager to find out our baby's gender, so I took a home gender test. Because it was hard to read, I took two tests, and it seemed that the tests showed we were going to have a little girl. I wanted to get one more test to confirm, but Doug cringed at the idea. The tests were a bit expensive, but in my impatient mind they were well worth the money! I had to wait for the first big ultrasound to get the real answer. When the 20 weeks finally passed, we went with great excitement to the doctor to find out if the gender tests were right. The tech finally asked, "Do you want to know the sex of your baby?" "Yes, yes, yes," I replied, unable to contain my zeal. The tech paused and said, "Look at the picture. What do you think it is?" "A girl?" I questioned, holding my breath for the answer. "It's a girl!" he exclaimed. I screamed "Yeeeeeeeeeeeeeeeeeeeeeeeees" at the top of my lungs. When I left the room and the nurse and staff saw me, I said, "Guess what we're having?" and they all replied, "We heard you screaming, so it must be a girl."

I could not have been more excited. Doug, on the other hand, looked a little afraid. The idea of a boy was easy for him to grasp. A girl—what was he going to do with a girl? When I brought home a truckload of pink to decorate her room, he had to sit down and adjust his eyes. He said, "I have a sister, and we never had this much pink for her." I replied with great joy and excitement, "Get used to it honey. Our little girl is going to be a princess!"

My pregnancy was wonderful. I had no complaints other than a few backaches. We had no indication the delivery would not be just like my delivery with Brady—easy.

Chapter Four
DELIVERY AND DISASTER

W e searched for the perfect name for our little girl. The two we liked the most were Lilianna and Gabriella. Lilianna means "resurrection" and Gabriella means "heroine of God." We did not settle on a name at that time because we thought that the moment we saw her, we would know which one suited her best. Little did we know that both names would be fitting.

I invited a roomful of women to be a part of the delivery. I wanted my baby to one day know that a team of amazing women were present at her birth and would continue to be by her side for life. I chose my mother, two sisters, and two friends, Brooke and Meghan. Brooke and Meghan are like little sisters to me and excellent examples of holy women who have overcome many obstacles.

The Last Thing I Remember

On July 27, I waddled uncomfortably into my 39-week checkup. My OB/GYN confirmed that all was well and sent me on my way, warning me to be watchful as I might deliver in the next few days. After the appointment, Doug and I drove over to my parent's house to eat chicken-fried steak—one of my favorites. We went to give my dad a gift since his birthday was the next day, July 28. During dinner, I began to feel some light contractions, but I was not sure if they were real or imagined. We went home, and as the night progressed so did my contractions. I called my mom to tell her she might get a call in the middle of the night. I was in labor!

That is the last thing I remember. Surreally, three-and-a-half months after coming home from the hospital, I found notes in my purse that I took while having contractions. I had charted each one—the time and distance apart. Even though my handwriting was on that piece of paper, I have no memory of writing it. It was an eerie feeling.

Re-Tell Me the Story

I was absent from the conscious memory of life for at least three days. In the days following my return home, I asked Doug to write his account of the delivery. At that time, my short-term memory was not strong, so even though he told me the story many times, I still could not fully grasp it. Having it written out, I thought, would help me piece it together myself. In addition, it would save him from reliving it over and over. We could also share it with the many people who had prayed for us and wanted to know the details of what had happened.

The following is a blog my dear husband, Doug, wrote and posted on the Foundation for Life and Love website after experiencing the most traumatic event of his life, an event that turned his whole world upside-down in a matter of minutes. This was how I found out what happened to me, and it is how I will share it with you.

Doug Pritchard, August 26, 2010

Around 4:30 a.m. my wife, Melanie, began to feel stronger contractions, a prelude to full-blown labor pains.

The culmination of months of appointments had finally arrived. We began the long trip from our home to the same hospital where my wife gave birth to our son just two-and-a-half years before. Once we arrived, we were taken to the triage room of the labor and delivery department, where the nurses determined that Melanie was far enough along to be admitted. Melanie and I hit the phones, contacting everyone we wanted present, as well as those close friends and family who could not be at the hospital, asking all to pray for us. For every contraction that occurred, Melanie offered her suffering and pain for the reparation and graces of many of our infirm or struggling loved ones and friends. It was beautiful and a marvel to see. It is something I recommend to all expectant mothers and fathers.

What happened in those early morning hours at the hospital were strikingly similar to the way things transpired for the birth of our son. There was no cause for concern as the labor progressed easily. Once we received a room, Melanie requested an epidural. Twenty minutes later, the anesthesiologist entered and relieved Melanie of the pain that had been growing significantly over the past couple of hours. She then updated many friends by text, praising the invention of localized anesthesia.

Around 6:00 a.m., Melanie's parents arrived at the hospital with news of who else was en route. As we waited patiently for the labor to progress, at 7:00 a.m. Melanie's OB/GYN arrived and informed us that things were moving rapidly and thus ruptured her bag of water. Melanie's two close friends Brooke and Meghan arrived. Melanie had asked them to join her own sisters and mother to witness the birth of our child. Meghan had stayed the night at our house to watch our son and bring him to the hospital when we called her. We were all in the room while the attending nurse reviewed some information with us and checked on my wife.

Melanie indicated she felt like something was wrong; she was light-headed and felt a little nauseous. At that point, my father-in-law took our son out of the room to prevent him from witnessing his mother being sick. By 7:30 a.m., Melanie said she felt like she might pass out. Immediately, the nurse and Meghan, who is also a nurse, attempted to reposition her and try to determine the cause of her light-headedness, as there was no indication from her vitals that something was amiss.

Then Melanie slumped to her side, and had what seemed like a mild convulsion. I was standing at the end of her bed when I witnessed her heart rate and blood pressure flash zero on her monitors. Our unborn child's heart rate began to plummet precipitously, too. As I looked at Melanie's face, her skin turned a deep blue. I knew then she was not breathing and had no heart rate. I had seen enough movies to know that this was not good.

I watched as a team of staff wheeled my wife out of the room two doors down to the operating room in an attempt to save her life as well as my daughter's. I said a simple prayer through my tears, "God, I know this is more than I can handle, which means you have a plan and a purpose in this, and I trust you. But please, if it is your will, allow me to hold my wife again." I have never felt more helpless and afraid in all my life.

I finished my prayer and saw that our family and friends were in shock and in tears as the next two people stepped into the room: the hospital social worker and a priest. I am almost ashamed to say my first thought was, "I am a widower. They have come to tell me my wife has died and they did everything they could." However, they just said, "Melanie is still in the O.R., and your baby was delivered and is in the nursery receiving attention." We all began to pray, holding hands and crying to God and all the saints in an appeal to save my wife's life.

The next person to come in was the general surgeon, who indicated that she happened to walk past the nurses' station right outside our door when the incident took place, so the response to the cardiac arrest was immediate. This most likely saved Melanie's life. The right person was in the right place at the right time. She told us that Melanie had entered the O.R. clinically dead—she had no pulse and was not breathing. The team shocked her with a defibrillator with no effect, began CPR, and then shocked her again. This resulted in a faint heartbeat. She was shocked a total of four times, and it took ten minutes for them to fully resuscitate her.

I went to the nursery to see my daughter. As I wiped the tears from my face to see her, the first thing I noticed was her blonde hair and light eyes, just like her mother's. At this time, I did not know if Melanie would live or die. When the nurses asked me the baby's name, I thought, "What would Melanie want me to name her?" I replied, "Gabriella," the "heroine of God." We had decided that if we named her Gabriella, then we would affectionately call her "Ella" during her younger years.

While I was in the nursery, an O.R. nurse entered and informed me that they had stabilized Melanie and were going to move her to ICU shortly.

The head of the ICU came to our room soon after and told us they thought Melanie had experienced an amniotic fluid embolism. This means that amniotic fluid escaped her womb, went into her bloodstream, and caused a cardiac arrest when it reached her heart.

In the ICU, we were told to prepare our good-byes as there was little likelihood that Melanie would survive. Melanie's family and I consoled one another and took our time sharing what we thought were our last moments with her, as we waited for her heart to fail again.

We were also told that Melanie was experiencing a condition called DIC. In her case, it meant that her blood was clotting erratically. The surgical team transfused her blood to remove the amniotic fluid-tainted blood, and as a result, the constriction of her blood vessels caused by the amniotic fluid, ceased. Unfortunately, the constricting inflammation had been keeping a severed uterine artery from bleeding; when it abated, the artery began to bleed freely into her now closed abdomen.

I found out later from other doctors that a uterine artery is often cut during an emergency Caesarean section, but it is caught and remedied instantly as it will bleed quickly and dangerously. In Melanie's case, very little blood appeared during the C-section, so no remedial action was taken.

By the time noon rolled around, Melanie had received vast quantities of blood- thickening products to assist in clotting. We did not know the artery was bleeding freely until Melanie's brother Larry, a cardiothoracic surgeon, identified it when he viewed her chart while she was in the ICU.

Another surgeon was called to perform a sonogram of her belly and confirmed that Melanie's belly was, indeed, full of blood. They needed to operate again immediately. The nurses and doctors indicated there was very little chance she would survive this surgery, so for a second time, we said our good-byes.

By now, we were all distraught. I never dreamed I would have to think of what to tell my spouse on her deathbed, let alone actually say it, more than once. I was the last to have time with her before the second surgery; I said simply this: "I love you. I will always love you. Brady and Ella are beautiful and love you. If you have any fight left, then fight. Despite my hopes, promise me that you will follow your guardian angel wherever he leads you. Where he leads you will be where God needs you."

Miraculously, Melanie survived this surgery as well. The doctors removed five liters of blood from her abdomen alone and were able to identify the source of the bleeding and packed down her belly (simply put, they stuffed her belly full of towels to compress the bleeding). They indicated that as a result of the amount of fluids given to her during the transfusions, she was very swollen, so they could not close her abdomen. When they brought her back to the ICU, she was open on her bed, increasing the risk of infection. I was elated that Melanie was still alive.

Larry informed me that they had stopped the bleeding and that pressure had been regained in her circulatory system. However, the issue now was that the multiple blood products given for most of the morning had thickened her blood to a consistency like molasses. This meant that her heart had to work three times as hard to pump blood through her system. My brother-in-law told me that she would experience heart and lung failure.

I waited and watched as what he said came true over the course of an hour. She had been on a ventilator since the initial operation early that morning, but now it was assisting at 100 percent; this meant that she was no longer assisting in her own breathing. Scans of her heart revealed her ejection fraction (or how well her heart was pumping) was only 5 percent (normal is between 55 percent and 65 percent). I prayed that her mentor, John Paul II, the man whose writing changed her life and who supplied the material for her work, would intercede for another morsel of grace in this day already filled with miraculously beaten odds.

It was then that I found a quiet place and wept as my wife was slipping away. I wept for my children, my family, and myself. One of my best friends, Kemi, from my small hometown in Missouri, walked into view. I gave him a hug and wept some more. I made a heart-wrenching phone call to my father before I went back into the ICU, where my in-laws, Kemi, and the priests, who had been close friends with Melanie since their college days, were waiting.

I noticed my brother-in-law was on his phone frequently, so I pulled him aside to ask what was happening. He said that he was planning a transport for Melanie to a more specialized hospital's critical care unit in case she needed artificial support. I told him I trusted his opinion and asked him to make it happen. He organized a "hospital on wheels" to come the hour from the specialized hospital to the hospital where we were to assess and transport her that night.

They arrived around 7:30 p.m. and told us that Melanie would not have to be put on a special type of heart and lung machine (ECMO) since her medications were stabilizing her enough for transport. Knowing that her heart and lungs were hanging on by threads, we said our good-byes for the third time. Melanie's sister, Kym, volunteered to stay with Ella so the rest of us could go with Melanie.

My friend drove me to the new hospital, and we arrived a few minutes before Melanie. We found more friends in the waiting room, one of whom handed me a pouch and told me to hold on to it as long as I needed it. I opened it to find a medium-sized crucifix with first class relics of five different saints (including Saints Paul of the Cross, Gemma, and Maria Goretti). By now it was about 9:00 p.m. Soon a team of doctors entered to discuss Melanie's case. Each one of the doctors and surgeons told us their plans for helping Melanie recover. They advised us that it might be too little, too late, and that even if she survived, she might have severe brain damage from the period of time her brain was without oxygen.

After the doctors' reported that she was stable and that nothing could be done until morning, we attempted to sleep wherever we could for the night in the waiting area. I awoke after about two hours of sleep to the news that Melanie would be having another operation, her third, to remove the packing from her open abdomen, to assess the damage and possible bleeding, and to close the wound.

Just prior to this operation, the ICU staff informed us that they would try to withhold some of the sedation so they could assess Melanie's neurological state more accurately. I had been told earlier in the day that if Melanie had experienced an amniotic fluid embolism, the fact that she survived the initial cardiac arrests was a miracle, but that the very few who do make it are likely to be permanently and severely neurologically impaired and perhaps brain-dead. So needless to say, I was again prepared for the worst, but prayed for another miracle.

As I entered Melanie's room with her sister, Kym, I saw that her eyes were open and looking around. I said, "Hey, babe." Without hesitation, she looked at me and her eyes began to well up with tears. I was elated, but I knew I did not have much time. I went immediately to her side. Her arms had been restrained to prevent her from taking out her ventilator tube or any other IVs or monitors. I told her I loved her and I was so proud of her. I tried to calm her down and asked her simple questions to which she nodded or shook her head. It was clear to me that, at that point, my wife was not brain dead or even neurologically impaired.

Kym saw this exchange and ran to the waiting room to get a picture of Ella for Melanie to see before she was taken to surgery. It might be the only opportunity for her to see her daughter if she did not make it through the risky operation. She came rushing back into the room with a picture of baby Ella on a BlackBerry. We showed it to Melanie and she began to cry. Twisting and turning, she tried to escape her bed. The nurses sedated her to calm her down so she did not cause any more medical problems as her abdomen was still open. As they wheeled her off to surgery, for the first time throughout all this, I felt some optimism and hope, despite the low probability of her survival.

Kym and I returned to the waiting room with smiles and tears streaming down our faces. We shared the experience with loved ones and friends and the mood was joyful and prayerful. I saw almost every person in the waiting room at one point or another whisper a quiet prayer of thanksgiving to God for further evidence of his mercy and grace in this situation. It was beautiful.

After about an hour, one of the operating nurses came to tell us that the surgery was going well, but the doctor anticipated it would take another hour or so to complete. I had already been asked to sign a consent form which, in the case of dire necessity, would allow for a full hysterectomy; that thought dwelled in my mind, although the surgeon had said that the chances of that happening were remote. I was not sure how Melanie or I would react if this great defender of the womb needed to have hers removed.

A little over an hour later, the surgeon consulted with my in-laws and me in a private room. He told us that everything had gone very well, that there was no additional bleeding, no hysterectomy, and no obvious infection despite the wound being open for almost 24 hours. I felt like Job in the face of doubtful friends holding on to his faith and trusting that God would not forsake a faithful servant—and Melanie is truly a good and faithful servant.

As a side note, the nurses who attended this surgery informed Melanie a few days later that in the 25 years they had worked in nursing, they had never seen anyone live through something like this. In fact, they told Meghan they had given Melanie a zero percent chance of survival.

With this surgery complete, her wounds closed, and her heart and lungs improving, a miraculous recovery began to occur. Within the next 24 hours, Melanie was weaned off all medications except those for pain. She was talking and was allowed to move from her bed to a recliner. I got word that her ventilator had been removed and she was breathing on her own while I was on the road between Melanie's hospital, Ella's hospital, and our friend's house where Brady was staying. I opted to let Kym continue to care for Ella at the other hospital because I wanted to be at Melanie's side to speak to her.

When I arrived, I immediately went to her room. Her father, a man I had never seen cry until this ordeal, was smiling from ear to ear with eyes full of tears. I sat next to my wife. She touched my face and said, "Hey, babe, how are you?" I laughed and kissed her hand and cried. I cried for joy and thanked God for his grace and for all the petitions offered from the whole Communion of Saints. Melanie's next words were profound, though she did not know it. She had seen another picture of Ella and told me, "It's okay, honey. You can take care of the kids by yourself." I knew she only meant she would need time to recover and would not be able to help as much as she would like, but my immediate response spoke to the severity of the situation she had just experienced. I quickly said, "I'm glad I don't have to."

With that, I left to let her rest, but of course with my wife that did not happen. She allowed the parade of family and close friends come to see her and continuously stated that she was going to "get out of here" soon. She was not quite clear about what she had been through and her short-term memory was barely intact—all normal difficulties for trauma patients in her situation. However, she regained her short-term memory within a couple of days. I woke up very early the next day and went to bring Ella home. As we were getting discharged, many of the nurses who had assisted us came to say hello and shared beautiful stories of prayer and told me how this situation had touched their lives deeply and permanently. It was amazing, and caused me to make my oft-repeated response to the overwhelming support and prayers: All glory to God and his great mercy!

Before going home, Ella and I went to see Melanie so that she could hold her for the first time. We walked through columns of friends and family in the waiting room eagerly anticipating the joy of this reunion. When I brought

Ella to Melanie, she began to cry. Though I knew that she would most likely not remember the event, I permanently etched that image in my mind and asked a friend to take a picture. I wanted her to see that moment and know that she was as happy and joyful as I had ever seen her.

From that day on, Melanie's recovery progressed rapidly. Aside from sleeping, Ella was with us at the hospital throughout the rest of Melanie's stay. Brady and Ella were now both back at our house under the watchful eyes of my mother, who had flown in from Missouri, and Melanie's mother and sister. On the morning of August 3, 2010, Melanie was discharged from the hospital to continue her recovery at home. Our world and the world of many others had changed significantly over those six days. I thought to myself how appropriate it was that Melanie would be allowed to rest at home beginning on the seventh day, her own resurrection of sorts. God is good!

The doctors informed us that Melanie would recover completely from the surgeries, but her heart function would take more time. They prescribed medication to help her heart recover and provided her with a portable defibrillator against the 50 percent chance that her heart would arrest again in the next three months. In follow-up appointments, many of the doctors we spoke to used the term "miraculous" more than once in our conversations. While that took me by surprise, I knew that what they could not explain, we could, thanks to faith.

Melanie's family was a tremendous help and supportive force throughout it all. I cannot understate the role of my own parents in this process and what they meant to me. Throughout every agonizing up and down, I consistently called my father to update him on Melanie's condition. My parents went about their normal days in Columbia, Missouri, and waited with baited breath to know the latest, while praying fervently. Then they both flew down to be with us and help take care of the children. It was the best feeling to hug my father and mother and feel their support.

Whether this event means Melanie will have to take a pill for the rest of her life to regulate her heart does not in any way cast a shadow of doubt on the series of miracles and graces that poured out upon her, our family, and the thousands of people who prayed and supported us! God allowed Melanie to be the lighthouse in this storm of life to bring many stranded souls back home to the heart of Jesus. I have been blessed that my wife and children are alive and well by God's grace.

The Strength of My Husband

Doug ended his blog this way:

All glory to God! Please continue to pray for us and especially pray for those families who have had similar experiences but with a different outcome. Pray for all families and mothers. Never stop praying!

After he wrote it, I read it, but at the time, it was still too early for me to truly understand the gravity of what had taken place. My mental function was weak. I do not think I even cried while reading it. When I re-read it a few months later, I sobbed in heartache and pain for what he had experienced. Doctors, friends, and family have all commented on the visible strength, faith, and calm my husband possessed during it all. As it turns out, he was a true inspiration for all of them and continues to be as we share our story with others.

Doug and I have been asked many times to share our story with audiences at conferences, on the radio, and on TV. January 2011, I appeared on EWTN's *Life on the Rock* program where I spoke about the incident as well as how

Doug and I met. I mentioned how Doug would read books about St. Joseph and had told me, "St. Joseph knew how to love a woman perfectly, and I think you deserve to be loved perfectly, so I am trying to learn how." A man from Italy saw the program and wrote this to me:

> I have returned to Jesus because of suffering through a separation from my wife of only ten years. I felt chills throughout my body when you described the little anecdote of when Doug practically confessed his total love for you. Could I please also ask you guys for the titles of the books Doug read on St. Joseph? I ask this of you because if my wife decides to return, I want to be ready to love the right way.

I was brought to tears thinking of this man's suffering and knowing Doug's words had brought him hope.

Doug exhibited great strength throughout the ordeal, but I could tell in the months that followed the great pain he continued to feel as he processed what had happened. Although I lived, he watched me die in front of his own eyes, an image he will never forget. I have witnessed how God has worked through Doug's suffering to bring him to a greater level of faith and trust in the Lord. Our relationship has become stronger as we have lived through something most people will never have to think about. I once told Doug that I wanted to have an "epic" love in our marriage that people could not help but talk about. Little did I know that I would get what I asked for just three years into our marriage. In light of what happened, we no longer want epic. We just want to live simply for the Lord.

Chapter Five

A MATTER OF THE HEART

*G*od knows all things. He knew this would happen to me and even permitted it to occur. God permits suffering in our lives for a greater purpose. He knew this would take place, and he made sure the right people were there to save me. What are the odds that the first major medical problem I experienced in 33 years would be heart failure, when my very own brother just happens to be a cardiothoracic surgeon who not only specializes in the heart, but is also an expert in heart failure? God knows all things!

Although my brother's name is Orazio Lawrence Amabile, we always affectionately called him "Larry." I never even knew his full name until I was 12. His wife and our mother are the only members of the family who call him Orazio. To write about my brother, I must call him by the name I grew to love him as, Larry. To the medical profession and his wife he can be known as Orazio, but to me, he will always be Larry.

Doctor "Larry" Amabile

Larry was not your average medical student. As a matter of fact, he never intended on becoming a doctor until he saw a trauma surgery at a hospital one Saturday night while completing an assignment for an EMT class he was taking to fulfill an elective he needed for college graduation.

As Larry witnessed the surgery, a desire came over him to become this kind of doctor, so he changed career directions. He had taken none of the required prerequisites in his undergraduate program, so his course-work started virtually from scratch. He managed to get into medical school and worked hard to become a doctor.

Becoming a heart surgeon was not something he had considered either, until the University of Arizona Medical Center contacted him after one of his rotations in their heart program and suggested it to him. The doctor there said my brother had easily picked up the knack for heart surgery, and wanted to offer Larry a fellowship. As many of you know, fellowships are hard to come by, so being handed one without even applying is a pretty big deal. He accepted it, and we were so proud!

Tucson Hero

In Tucson, Larry began his career as an Assistant Professor of Cardiothoracic Surgery at the University of Arizona Medical Center. While driving to lunch one day, he witnessed a drive-by shooting. Without a second thought, he followed the injured victim's car and when the car stopped, the injured man exited to lie down on a porch where he was bleeding to death. My courageous brother picked him up, put him into an ambulance (which he already directed to the location), and placed two life-saving chest tubes into his thorax to release pressure and allow him to breathe. Larry contacted the O.R. and had a room readied for the man. When they got to the E.R., though, the patient lost his vital signs. My brother began CPR while wheeling him into the O.R.; then he immediately operated on him to save his life. The Tucson Police Department presented Larry with an award of recognition for his courage and heroism in a scene of danger. Shortly after, my brother made a bold decision to make a name for himself in Phoenix, closer to his family.

Coming Home

Larry had lived away from Phoenix for about 13 years while in medical school and surgical training, so the family celebrated his return home. In May 2009, he accepted a position as a cardiothoracic surgeon with Phoenix Cardiac Surgery. In November 2009, he became the first surgeon in Phoenix to perform a PTE (pulmonary thromboendarterectomy), which required him to put a patient into a deep hypothermic circulatory arrest. Basically, that means that he put the patient on ice to cool his body temperature to 18 degrees Celsius and stopped his heart and blood flow throughout his body for 40 minutes while he removed massive clots in the patient's lungs. Larry was featured on local news stations as well as on FOX local and national news. He was also recognized in the Arizona Republic for pioneering this major surgery in Phoenix. Because of these heroic deeds, a few months before I gave birth, Larry's wife Remi and I nominated him for the Phoenix Business Journal's Health Care Hero Award, and he was selected as a finalist.

Little did my brother know that one day his own little sister would experience heart failure and he would be our family's source of hope. Here is his account of his participation in my unlikely survival.

Orazio (Larry) Amabile, November 18, 2010

I have been looking forward to this time of my life for many years. My first child was about to be born. Ironically, our son was due the same day as Melanie's daughter, so I was excited to have someone to share this new adventure with my wife and me. I had dreams of play dates and birthday parties together, and hoped that these two cousins would forge a great friendship.

On July 17, Remi had an OB/GYN appointment at which we were informed that she had a low amniotic fluid index. Since I am in the medical field, I know this can cause some consequences between the child and mother, so it put me on edge. The doctor said it was not much to worry about, but that if it dropped, they would have to induce her. At our next appointment, we learned that the amniotic fluid index was lower and that the umbilical cord was wrapped around our son's neck two times, so this heightened my anxiety level. As a surgeon, I have trained in obstetrics; I knew that when things go wrong in obstetrics, they go bad really fast.

With so many factors to consider, her OB/GYN decided to admit her and induce labor. The next 24 hours were the scariest for me. I was constantly worried and trying to make sure nothing was missed. After 24 hours of hard labor and exhaustion, my worst fears came true. The baby was not descending and the cord was still wrapped around his neck, so Remi was taken to the O.R. for a C-section. Thank God everything turned out okay. Lorenzo arrived on July 23 at 5:30 a.m., just two days before my 40th birthday. He weighed 8 pounds, 1 ounce. Melanie was at the hospital with us the entire time, waiting for her nephew to be born and anticipating having her own child soon.

The next five days, I was the happiest dad in the world with the excitement of my new baby and my wife doing well—that is, until I received a phone call on the morning of July 28, just a few hours after Melanie had texted me she was in labor and was doing fine. The phone call came at 7:30 a.m. and abruptly woke me up after I was up all night with my little one. On the line was my mother, hysterically crying. I could not make out what she was saying, but I did hear, "Melanie is dying. Melanie is dying." Instantly, images went through my mind. All were bad—images of families and doctors crying as I thought back to obstetrical disasters I had witnessed in the past. My worst fear as a physician was coming true.

I got dressed immediately, jumped in my car, and raced toward the hospital 40 miles away. It was the longest 40 miles I have ever driven. I got back on the phone with my mom and she said they took Melanie to the operating room and were still performing CPR on her. During the drive, I talked to God. In fact, for the whole 30-minute drive, I cursed him. I said, "Don't you take her! I will hate you forever. I'm not ready for her to go." I had feelings of hate and began to doubt God's existence. How could he snatch such a God-fearing woman and her child from existence the way he was doing? Melanie was a woman who believed in him, loved him, obeyed him, and he was taking her life. That was not supposed to happen to people like her, so at that point in my mind I doubted the existence of God.

Another reason I felt this way was because I have stood over bodies whose families prayed for their loved ones, but they still died. I always thought this happened to other families, but never to mine. As I finally parked the car and raced up to the O.R., I found many of my family members crying in the hallway. Melanie was nowhere in sight. Disregarding all signs that said "Personnel Only" or "Keep Out," I found a nurse and asked what was happening. Looking toward the door where Melanie was, the nurse said Mel was going in and out of ventricular fibrillation, and had to get shocked several times. She said they were doing everything they possibly could. I wanted to know everything—what her blood pressure was, what her heart rate was, and what drips she was on. I wanted to know this because I knew no one could take care of her the way I could. Now I know what it was like to be the physician of a family member who is dying, which probably was annoying to the staff working on her.

I peeked into the room. There were 10 to 12 doctors and nurses feverishly working hard to keep Mel alive. After about 30 minutes of resuscitation, Mel's blood pressure stabilized enough to move her to the ICU. My big fear was that because she had been without oxygen for so long, my bright, sweet, caring, loving sister would have suffered irreversible neurologic injury. The minute she got into the ICU, I went to her bedside, stroked her hair, and whispered in her ear, "I am here now, and I will take care of you." I immediately got to know her chart and condition.

As I looked at her chart and saw her trends, I concluded she was bleeding internally. Her body was developing multiple organ failure and she had been massively transfused. I immediately spoke to the intensivist and said, "She is bleeding internally. You need to call the obstetrician and get her back in the O.R." About 30 minutes to an hour later, Mel was rushed back to the O.R., where a general surgeon performed an exploratory surgery. The surgeon found that the uterine artery had been cut during the C-section and was freely bleeding. They tied off the artery, but by this point, Melanie's blood was so thin that they had to pack her with lap-pads in order to keep her from bleeding to death just from the raw surfaces on her body.

By this time, Mel had received over 31 units or more of blood products. She was transferred back to the ICU and was so massively volume-overloaded that it was very difficult to oxygenate her blood, even with the ventilator set to maximum. After looking at the x-ray and labs, I thought to myself, "Her heart is failing." I told the intensivist we needed to get an echocardiogram (ECHO) to confirm my suspicion. They came with the ECHO machine and we found Melanie's heart's ejection fraction was five percent, normal is sixty percent. As I stared at the screen and before taking any medical action, I decided to call a colleague and friend who is the chief of cardiothoracic surgery at a specialized hospital nearby. I told him my sister was at a small community hospital where she was actively dying. I also informed him that the intensivist was doing his best to keep her alive with his limited resources. I also knew in my mind that it was possible that Mel might need an artificial heart. My colleague said he would immediately come with his team and bring an ECMO circuit to support both her lungs and heart, which were both failing.

At that point, I informed the other physicians Melanie might need biventricular support (ECMO), which they could not offer her at this hospital. While the team from the other hospital was en route, the intensivist and I worked feverishly to medically manage Melanie and we somewhat stabilized her.

My colleague showed up with his surgical team in an ambulance and an unmarked car. By this time on high doses of heart medicine, Melanie's blood pressure stabilized, but her heart was still working very hard. The team picked Mel up and transferred her to the new hospital, where they thought she would possibly undergo placement of two heart blood pumps. Upon arrival, special pressure catheters were placed in her heart and the arteries of her lungs to monitor her heart function beat by beat. The next day, she was taken to the operating room, where they removed the packing from her abdomen and closed her belly. It had been opened and exposed for the day.

Over the next four days, Melanie's heart started to recover from the initial insult. It was amazing how she continued to stay stable even while her heart's ejection fraction rate was still severely depressed. In the following days, she was transferred out of ICU to the telemetry floor, where she continued to recover and was finally discharged and sent home.

I am grateful my sister and my niece did not suffer a terrible fate. I have been blessed to have both of them alive.

Now my son will have a playmate, and I will still have my sister to laugh with and to share our children's lives. As for my thoughts about God, I have not completely reconciled them. I do not know where my faith lies, yet. Was this an act of God or an act of medicine? I would like to believe it was God.

My Brother, My Hero

My brother really is a true hero. Had he not been bold enough to make a new start in a new practice, he would not have been able to rush to the hospital to be by my side, but God knew all things. God put it on Larry's heart to come home. As I read his struggle with seeing how God was working in this, I understand his doubts, as his heart was in anguish and pain from the situation. As God has used this incident to bring others back to him, it is my prayer that God will allow my brother to see his presence in the incident and in Larry's own life with great clarity in time.

Just two and a half weeks after returning home from the hospital, the Phoenix Business Journal held their Health Care Heroes award breakfast. Even though I was still in a lot of pain, on a ton of medication, and wearing a portable defibrillator, Kym and I went. I wanted to be there for my medical hero. All four finalists had pretty amazing and heroic stories. I thought my brother had a chance at winning until they spoke about how one of the other finalists rescued people from the rubble in Haiti. I knew at that moment that Larry would walk away as a finalist instead of the winner. Regardless, the fact that he was a finalist was still a huge honor. They did not have to tell me he was a winner for me to know it in the depths of my heart. If they had only known of his latest heroic deed, helping to save my life just a few weeks before the ceremony, they might have reconsidered.

God Knew All Things

When I think of my brother now, I feel safe. Through my recovery, I have bombarded him with phone calls about every ache and pain I have felt, worried there was something else wrong with me. He answered every call right away and assured me every time that he would see me through. He checked up on me constantly to make sure I obeyed all doctors' orders. Words cannot express the gratitude I have for my brother and his expertise in medicine.

The Lord permitted my heart to fail, but he did not leave me stranded and alone. He fashioned my very own brother not only to be one of the most promising heart surgeons in the nation, but he also brought Larry home to Phoenix. He allowed Larry's wife to give birth to their son five days before Ella to ensure that Larry would be off work when this happened to me. Surgeons are very busy and often my brother travels to Flagstaff to work on hearts there, too. For him to be 100 percent available to drop everything and be by my side in a matter of minutes is a miracle in itself. But God knew all things and he set all things in motion. He knew it when he formed us in our mother's womb.

As I mentioned earlier, I was frustrated and suffered heartache because it took so long for me to get pregnant. I even tried to control my fertility, doing anything morally possible to help myself get pregnant. Even when I took fertility enhancing drugs, I still did not get pregnant. In the midst of it all, I held on to the belief that God had a plan and even though I might not understand it, it must be for the best. Even the fertility specialist suggested I might never have children again. Only God knew his plan. Had I gotten pregnant even a month earlier, all the things that needed to happen for my survival might not have been in place. God knew all things and set all things in motion before this tragedy came to pass. This has been a great lesson in trusting the plans of God in place of my own. He knows best!

Chapter Six
THE REST OF THE STORY

*I*t was exciting to get pregnant at the same time as Remi. She is more than a sister-in-law; she truly is a sister to all of us girls. In addition to Larry, I also have two sisters. It is hard for a woman to marry into a family full of girls. No matter who my brother brought home, I did not like her. I always thought he could do better, but I am sure that is how most little sisters feel. But Remi–she was different. There is not a soul in the world who could not like Remi. She is kind, loving, and so accepting, and the way she looks at my brother is beautiful. I can tell she truly loves, respects, and adores him and wants nothing more than to make him happy. Each person in our family always comments on their gratitude that Larry picked a woman who was so easy for all of us to love so much! She fits right into our family.

What Larry Left Out

After Remi read Larry's account, she sent me her own. "I think your brother hid a little of this in his story, and I thought you should know the rest of the story." Her account has helped me to connect the pieces in my mind and allowed me to experience more of what my brother was feeling emotionally—things he never shared with the rest of the family. Only Remi had access to that kind of information.

Remi Amabile, December 2, 2010

Who would ever have imagined two sisters in the same family could get pregnant at the same time and have the exact same due date? What are the chances? Yes, Melanie and I were both due on August 4. We were so excited and were competing for the first delivery. This was so funny because I remember Melanie toward the end, walking around the mall and trying her best to get her baby out before me.

But instead, on July 23 at 5:30 a.m., our baby boy entered the world. Everyone was so happy. He was healthy, I was recovering well, and mommy and daddy were on cloud nine. We had also just celebrated Orazio's 40th birthday. Melanie had made chocolate cupcakes and the whole family surprised him with a little party in my hospital room.

In the very early morning on July 28, Melanie sent us a text message saying she was at the hospital in labor and everything was going well. At some point later, she also called Orazio to let him know all was well and we did not need to be there since we had our new little one. A couple of hours later, Orazio's phone rang, and I heard him say "What?" Then he jumped out of bed and started getting dressed. I asked him what was going on, and he said Melanie had passed out. Then the phone rang again, and he said, "I'll be right there," and then he hung up and said, "Melanie is dying." I started to cry. My mom and dad were visiting, so I ran to their bedroom and woke them up and said "Melanie's dying, please come pray with me." They got up right away. We had no idea what was going on. We were just shocked and in disbelief.

I kissed Orazio goodbye and he left. I was so worried about him having to drive 40 miles by himself in that state of mind. I wanted to go with him, to be there for him. Most importantly I wanted to be there for Melanie, but it was impossible for me to make the drive so soon after my

C-section and having my newborn. I felt terrible—she had been there for me during my labor, and she even had her friend, Father John Parks, come to see me and pray with me while I was in labor. I was crying so hard my C-section was causing me pain. I couldn't control it. I wanted to get in my car and drive to the hospital, but I couldn't. My mom and dad asked me what happened and I said, "I don't know. Let's just pray the rosary." We started praying and waiting to hear something.

When Orazio finally called me, it was worse than I imagined. He first said the baby was okay, but that Melanie had coded—her heart failed—twice and was bleeding to death. He said she was in DIC; she had lost all her blood volume and was unable to clot. I asked him if she was going to be okay and he said, "I don't know, Remi. She's in bad shape." Part of me thought he was exaggerating a little. I know from the past that he would give the worst-case scenario when it might not be as dire as he made it sound. I thought to myself, "Yes, that had to be it. It couldn't be as bad as he says it is."

Later that day, I heard Orazio's truck pull up. I thought, "Maybe she's doing better?" When he walked in the door, we all looked up at him waiting for him to say something. He walked over to the couch where I was sitting and I remember thinking that he looked like he had aged 10 years. He looked so tired, as if the life had been sucked out of him. He plopped down next to me, put his head on my shoulder, and cried. I began crying, too, and asked him if Melanie was okay. I could not understand much of what he said because he was crying so hard, but I heard him say she was very sick.

After a few minutes, he got up and went down the hall. I waited a little bit and then went to look for him. I found him in our son Lorenzo's room, sitting on the rocking chair with his hands on his face, sobbing. I went to comfort him. He kept saying "My little sister, my little sister," over and over. Orazio and I had been together for over 10 years, and I had never seen him in such pain and agony. It was the most heart-breaking thing I have ever seen. I knew how helpless he must have felt as a doctor being unable to do anything to help his sister.

He laid down on the bed and closed his eyes when the phone rang. It was one of the doctors saying they were taking Mel back into the o.r. to find the origin of the bleeding. He got up, kissed Lorenzo and me goodbye, and left again. I thought, "This can't be happening. Melanie is such a good person, truly one of God's people. Why is this happening to her?" I could not imagine life without her in it.

Later, I got a text from Orazio that said, "Called colleague, he's coming down to put Melanie on ECMO." I knew what that meant. She was dying and this was their last ditch effort to save her. "Oh God, please do not take her," I prayed. I told my parents and we prayed another rosary.

Then Orazio called me and said they were transferring Mel to a more specialized hospital. He also said that he and the intensivist began massively medicating her to get her heart to start working a little—and miraculously it was working! For now, she would not need the ECMO. Thank you, GOD!! I started to have faith that she was going to be okay. He did not sound so doom and gloom; there was a little hope in his voice this time.

Once Mel had arrived safely at the new hospital and been set up in the ICU, Orazio came home. This, too, made me hope that she was going to be okay. He tried to eat, but could only take a few bites. He was still worried sick about Mel. He said she was nowhere near better, but he was relieved to have her at a hospital where they could put her on whatever device she would need to keep her alive if they needed to.

Orazio left again to check on Mel and then, once he felt comfortable, came home for the night. He had just fallen asleep when Lorenzo woke up to eat and for some strange reason, Orazio got up to feed him. I peeked in on them and saw him admiring his little boy, with tears streaming down his face. He told me how precious life was, and to savor every minute because you never know what could happen next.

The next day, we all went to visit Mel at the hospital. By the time we arrived, the doctors were getting ready to pull the tube from her throat to see if she could breathe on her own. What a miracle! Once they did that, Orazio took me back to see her. She was so swollen I did not even recognize her. I grabbed her hand and said, "Hi Mel. It's Remi. I love you so much, little sis." She looked at me and then at Orazio and he asked her, "Do you know who that is?" Melanie nodded her head yes very slightly.

I sat next to her and held her hand as Orazio and the other doctors talked about how well she was doing. I said to her, "You know, your brother saved your life. He's your hero, isn't he?" She looked at him and a tear rolled down her cheek. I got up and walked out of the room to cry; it broke my heart to see her that way. She looked terrible. Orazio came out to comfort me and assured me she looked a lot better than before, and that he believed she was going to be okay. I wiped my tears, went back in her room, and sat with her for a little while longer until it was time for more tests.

The next day, my mom, dad, and I went to visit her. She had been transferred into another room. She was talking slowly, and it seemed like we had to repeat things a lot. She asked about Lorenzo. She held Ella and said, "This is my Ella." I wanted to cry again; that was the picture I had prayed to see, Mel holding her baby girl, and there she was holding her. It was a beautiful miracle.

As each hour and day passed, Mel got better and better. I could not believe it! I knew Orazio was still worried about her. He questioned whether her heart was going to recover or if she would need a heart transplant down the road, and whether she had suffered any brain injury during the time she had "died." All these things he still worried about even though the rest of us were just ecstatic that she was alive. He never stopped worrying, which meant I never stopped worrying.

I remember the day I knew Mel was going to be fine. My mom and I had gone to a Mass that Melanie's friend Father Muir celebrated at her house four days after she came home. After the Mass, she wanted to know if she could do something. She called Orazio and asked him and he said, "No!" She called him a "dirt bag," something she called him when he was mean to her. At that moment, I knew Melanie had been given back to us.

Right Where She Needed to Be

To know that my strong, usually joy-filled brother was crying and hurting the way Remi described is hard to hear. Larry had the weight of the world on his shoulders that day (being a highly qualified cardiac surgeon) while I was experiencing severe heart and lung failure. This must have been the scariest thing for him to go through, knowing my imminent risk of death. All he could do was trust my doctors and hope they would heed his advice. This partnership between my brother and the physicians is the reason I survived. I cannot tell you how much appreciation I have for the doctors at the first hospital for seeing the wisdom in my brother and allowing him to advise them. I know Remi must have been going out of her mind being unable to come to the hospital. But she was right where she needed to be, taking care of her baby so Larry did not have to be worried about anything else. Her prayers were the most important thing she could have done for me that day! Her prayers, and the prayers of others, were like an arrow launched straight into the heart of this tragedy, and they were heard!

Chapter Seven
Through My Parent's Eyes

I am the youngest of four, the baby of the family. Larry and my sister, Kari, were born of my mother's first husband. Seven years after they married, they divorced. Later, my mother met and married my father and they had my sister, Kym, and me, thirteen months apart. My parents loved us equally. I never considered Larry and Kari as half-siblings and I do not even think I remember learning that information until I was a teenager. My mom was their mom and in every way possible, other than blood, my dad was their dad. We are very close-knit and enjoy each other's company. All of us kids seek out my mom and dad's wisdom in many of the decisions we make.

My Dad: Better Than Best, Greater Than Great...

Before I was married, my dad was the man I called for everything. "Hey, dad, can you fix my brakes? Can you come over and fix my sink? Can you come get me? I have a flat tire." No matter what it was, he would drop everything to come to my rescue. He is a special man and a special kind of father. There was never a day I did not know my father loved me because he always made sure I knew.

My earliest memories are falling asleep at night on the couch when I was about five. My dad would come in and gently lift me up in his arms and carry me off to bed to tuck me in. On the walk through the hall to my room, he would see my eye peek open, and say, "Who's better than best, greater than great, smarter than smart, faster than fast?" "You are, dad!" I would respond enthusiastically. Then he would get a serious look on his face and say, "No. You are, Melanie Welsch, and don't you ever forget it!"

Then he would ask, "Who's going to be the next astronaut?"

I responded, "I am!"

"Who's going to be the next doctor?"

"I am!"

"Who's going to be the first woman president of the United States?"

"I am!" I would say as if I really believed it. Every night before I went to bed, I was told I was better than best, greater than great, smarter than smart, faster than fast. I grew up believing that the sky was the limit and that I could be anything I wanted....I could even be the first woman president!

As a parent now, my husband and I took that model from my father and have our own phrase we say to Brady and Ella every night. "You are unrepeatable, irreplaceable, and unique. The day you were born, the world changed for the better because you are in it. There never was or ever will be anyone like you because you are special."

I know the positive effect my father's words had on me and want my children to grow up hearing how wonderful they are every day, too. My father's words built great confidence in me as a child and I hope mine have the same effect on my own children.

My Mom

There are not too many people whom I seek approval from in life, but my mother is one of them. She is my biggest supporter. When I was a child, she was always my mother, never my friend. She knew her role and was not afraid to lay down the law so that I might grow to be the woman she knew I could be. Now as an adult, she is still my mother; but in a really special way, she is my friend… my best friend. Doug laughs at me because I call her at least three times a day! I value her opinions and thoughts and greatly respect her. She is always there by my side.

My mother was in the room with me the entire 24 hours I was in labor with Brady. He was the first grandchild she ever saw born. I invited her again to watch the delivery of her new granddaughter. She may have thought I asked for her sake. But I must admit, I had more selfish reasons. I knew if she were there, I would feel calm and assured because she gives me strength. When she is around, I know everything will be all right. My dear mother was in the room when I died.

My Parent's Account

The following is my parent's account of nearly losing their youngest daughter. My mother wrote it on behalf of the two of them.

Sherry Welsch, October 25, 2010

We woke up to a phone call around 6:00 a.m. It was Melanie. She and Doug were at the hospital, in labor, and they were admitting her. We immediately got dressed and headed there. We did not want to miss seeing our granddaughter's birth, especially since it was my husband's birthday. We arrived at the hospital and were so excited that

Mel was on her way to becoming a mom again. Just then, Jim's sister Corrine called to wish him a happy birthday. He told her that Melanie was going to have her baby and she reminded him that their dad had died on this day. Jim said to me, "Well, at least this birthday will be better than the one when my father died."

Everything was going smoothly when all of the sudden, Melanie fell over as if she was having a seizure. It was like everything was in slow motion…the head nurse and others came and asked us to step outside. I watched them push her bed out the door and down the hall to the operating room. We were not sure what was going on; we knew it was not good, but we did not know exactly what had happened. The nurse asked us to stay in the waiting room. I responded, "I am not going anywhere. This is my daughter, and I'm not leaving!"

They brought us back into her labor room where we immediately held hands, said prayers for Mel, and cried. Jim and I stepped out in the hallway by the nurses station and saw one of the doctors from the operating room. She looked us in the eyes and said, "Your daughter is dying. If you want to say goodbye to her, you must do it now. You can go see her when she gets transferred to the ICU." Our hearts were devastated. We could not accept this news. I called my son and told him that something was wrong with Melanie, that it was very bad, and he needed to be here. I knew he could find out what was wrong and explain it to us. I called Kari and told her what had happened. Then I called Craig, my son-in-law, to find out when Kym had left Tucson. I wanted to know how long it would be before she got to the hospital. I told him what had happened, but asked him not to tell Kym while she was on the road. I was afraid that if she knew, she would take chances in order to get here faster. I could not handle having another child in danger. Then I called everyone in my cell phone list, begging for prayers. We were relieved when Orazio arrived.

My husband thought of his dad dying thirty-three years ago on his birthday and wondered, "Was God going to allow my daughter to die this day, too?" After some time, a social worker came and told us that Melanie had suffered a cardiac arrest, and they spent about ten minutes resuscitating her; she explained that Melanie had an amniotic fluid embolism. She said the baby was fine and asked Doug if he wanted to see her. He went to the nursery, then sent the social worker back to ask if I wanted to see baby Gabriella. Of course!!

Gabriella was so beautiful. I looked at Doug and thought what a wonderful father and son-in-law he was. I think of him as my son. If this was devastating to us, what was he feeling? Was he going to have to raise his two children without Melanie?

It was a conflicting time. We were joyful at the birth of our granddaughter and unbearably sad at possibly losing a daughter. We realized we may never be able to tell our daughter again how much we loved her and how much happiness she had brought into our lives. We were truly not prepared for the rollercoaster ride that we were about to go on beginning that first day. We went from extreme happiness to extreme sadness over and over again during that time.

Soon we were escorted to the ICU. With tears pouring down our faces and pain in our voices, we told Melanie we loved her and said goodbye. As we sat there with her, we were perplexed why God had let this happen to Mel. She was God's advocate, teaching and training young and old alike about God and about how precious life is and how we need to protect the babies in the womb as well as the older folks who some think have no value anymore. I told God that I was confused, but I trusted in him. I had to trust God, but I was not sure what he was going to allow Melanie to endure. Would he let her die or would he save her? It was very difficult to keep the faith during something devastating like this. I might have seemed calm, but there was havoc going on inside me. I prayed for the doctors and nurses who were working so hard to save her.

By the time we went back to the waiting room the hospital had provided for us, friends of Melanie had come to pray for her. Seeing her friends in despair, my husband announced to the group, "What happens to Mel is in God's hands, and we have to accept whatever it will be." All day, more people came until the halls were full of people praying. Friends brought relics of saints. I took them to Mel and touched her with each one, praying for their intercession.

Orazio was monitoring everything the doctors did. We felt more confident now. He would keep us well informed. They decided to take Mel back to surgery and I thought, "How can she survive this after everything else she has been through today?" The doctors were not optimistic. More prayers!

Mel came back from surgery and I stood by her bed and just put my fingers through her hair, hoping she somehow would know I was with her. As a small child and even as an adult she loved having my fingers comb through her hair. I told her to fight, that she must fight this.

Outside her room, I saw new faces of more friends who had come to pray. Seeing all these people gave us such hope. I truly believe this was how we made it though this difficult time. I kept saying, "God, please help her. I promise I will tell her the first talk she gives should be on the power of prayer." Jim went to the waiting room and saw the hopeless-looking crowd and said, "I am MAD! The evil one has thrown everything he has against my daughter, and she is still alive, and is going to live." He was no longer going to accept the grim thought that Melanie was going to die. Everyone who heard him called out, "Yes!" Feelings of hope began to spread. We were no longer going to believe that the worst would happen.

Throughout this ordeal, the hospital staff went above and beyond any expectations we had. They were at our side all day, keeping us informed. Melanie's delivery nurses sent down an angel statue and the hospitality staff sent flowers. They allowed Melanie's friends to pray outside her room, in the halls of the ICU. They never told us to be quiet or that there were too many people there. The nurses and staff even prayed along with us. Even though I broke down and cried on many occasions, the prayers sustained me.

When Melanie arrived at the new hospital, we waited in the waiting room until they allowed us to see her. She was still on a breathing machine and unconscious.

Many wonderful friends of Melanie and Doug came to the hospital over the next few days. Even though they were not able to see her, they stayed and prayed and kept us company. Jim's two sisters and niece flew down from Minnesota and his brother came to offer support. My nephew and his wife drove from Albuquerque to be with us. Sarah and Shelly, two of Melanie's bridesmaids, flew in to be with her. What a comfort they were to all of us. Lerry and Diane, Remi's parents, brought homemade burritos for everyone at the hospital. In addition, the Henry family brought coffee and bagels in the morning and sandwiches in the afternoon. They wanted to make sure all of us had something to eat. I have never experienced this kind of sacrifice from people I barely knew. How wonderful is our God? He sent us prayer warriors and sustained us with nourishment.

When the doctors were going to take Mel off the breathing machine and off some of the medications so she would awaken, we were warned that there was a chance she may not have all her faculties, since she had been without oxygen for some time when she had the cardiac arrest. I remember thinking, "Melanie is so smart that if she lost some faculties, she'd still be smarter than most!"

A day later, Gabriella was released from the hospital and Doug and Kym brought her to Melanie for the first time.

That was pure joy!! Brady was brought to the hospital as well. We were all together again.

When Melanie finally did awaken, Jim kissed her and said, "This is the most beautiful kiss I have ever had." When I spoke to her, she said, "Momma, did I have a stroke?" I told her, "No." Then I told her what really happened. Melanie's short-term memory was not intact, so throughout the next couple of days she asked the same questions over and over. After she asked many times about a stroke, I finally asked, "Melanie, why do you think you had a stroke?" She responded, "Because I am slurring my words." I responded, "Honey, if you had a stroke, you wouldn't be able to sit up in a chair and move as you are." That was the moment it finally stuck in her memory because she never asked again.

Words cannot reflect the pure horror of what it is like to almost lose a child. To this day, even though I am so grateful for the prayers that sustained us, my heart weeps. I still tear up and cry when I talk about it. Even though I know in my heart that God worked a miracle in saving Melanie and Gabriella through the many doctors and nurses who used their skill and through all the prayers said on their behalf, I still hurt. I suspect and hope that one day my heart will not weep. When everything was over and Melanie was recovering, Jim said, "My birthday will no longer be the day my dad died, but the day my daughter and granddaughter survived."

My Parents Devised a Plan

I speak about my father often in my talks. He has always been so motivational in his words to me growing up, my own pep rally of sorts. Many of my friends who were at the hospital told me he was so positive and uplifting that his optimism rallied and motivated the troops! When I think of what he was going through, what I find most notable was his bold statement to my friends and family to trust in God. Here my father was, totally helpless, but in the face of the suffering he was experiencing, he called upon the Heavenly Father to take charge.

My mother came daily to care for me and the children once I was released from the hospital. She saved my sanity. My mother retired when I was pregnant with Ella because she wanted to help Remi and me with our newborn children. However, plans had to change. With me in the state I was in, needing around-the-clock care, she had to divert all her attention to me. My mom and dad devised a daily plan. My mother came and stayed with me while my father went to help out Remi, then he would come see me when he had time. He would also visit my grandma Doris (my mom's mom), who was recently diagnosed with lung cancer, and my grandfather (my mom's dad), who was extremely ill and needed someone at his side to make sure he ate his meals every day.

When friends would come to give my mother a break for a couple hours on some days, she would run around town visiting her mother, father, and Remi, and then be back to take care of me. As much as she tried to conceal her heartache and pain, I could see her suffering daily as she dealt with so many hard circumstances at the same time. She cried a lot. We were able to talk through a lot of what was going on and drew strength from our own prayers as well as all those who prayed and were still praying for us. My parents' faith and strength were tested but they never doubted God; they continued to see his face in each day, in each struggle.

Chapter Eight

WIND BENEATH MY WINGS

*A*s these stories from my family began to help me connect the dots about my untimely death and revival, I had to know more about sweet Ella. What happened to Ella? The only thing I knew was that Kym had stayed with her while everyone went with me to the other hospital.

Kym and I are thirteen months apart, so during our younger years we often fought over toys, clothes, the car we shared, and much of what most sisters that close in age argue about. Even though we battled about such things, we always had each other's back. She was my big sis and everyone at school knew it. I followed in her footsteps by joining whatever club she was a part of and took the honors classes she took. She was the student body vice-president; when she graduated, I ran for the position and won. She showed me the ropes and took care of me. She was my comfort and protector at school. She even forgave me when I embarrassed her and myself beyond belief.

My Most Embarrassing Moment

The student body vice-president at my high school was in charge of the pep assemblies and one of the duties was to be the emcee. Having just been elected my junior year, the student council asked me to announce the winner of Winter Courts King and Queen Royalty as a way to prepare me for what to expect my senior year. I agreed to do it before it dawned on me that I was going to have to speak in front of 1400 of my peers. Terrified at the thought of it, I sought some advice. A wise person told me the best way to get over this fear was to practice in front of a mirror every day.

Before the assembly began, a student council member told me who the winners were in case the envelope got lost. The time for my announcement came fast. I walked out to the center of the gym and saw a sea of faces staring at me. I became terror-stricken. Nothing had prepared me for the way I felt. My stomach was in my throat and butterflies had been unleashed under my skin. Shaking, I grabbed hold of the microphone and it made a loud screeching noise that caught the audience's attention. All eyes were on me. I did not know how I was going to get words to exit my mouth. Then I remembered all the times I had practiced in front of the mirror. I took myself back to that happy place and said exactly what I practiced countless times before.

Things were going fine until they handed me the envelope to announce the winners. I tried to open it, but it seemed like it was super-glued shut. Maybe my palms were too sweaty to grip it or maybe my hands just could not stop shaking. It is all a blur. As I became increasingly nervous, some mean kids from the stands…you know the ones… the class clowns…the bullies…the smart alecks…started yelling out, "Hurry up! Open the envelope! What is taking so long?" I wanted to run out of there and never return. The envelope would not budge, so I just went back to the happy place in front of the mirror and said what I had practiced. "And the winners are Nathan Downs and Kym Welsch." Some student council members started crowning the new royalty when I realized something disturbing. MY SISTER DID NOT WIN!

For a split second, I thought about not saying anything and just running far, far away; but as if in slow motion, the palm of my hand went up to signal "STOP" and I yelled into the mic, "STOP, THE WINNER IS NOT KYM WELSCH. I MADE A MISTAKE. THE WINNER IS AMY." The crowd was in utter disbelief. They went from cheering to booing me in a matter of seconds. Confused, the student council members took the crown from my sister's head and put it on Amy's, de-robed her and gave the robe to Amy, and then grabbed the flowers from her arms and handed them to Amy.

My peers were relentless. It felt as though all 1400 students hated me. I looked at my parents, who seemed to be in shock. I felt as though my life as a high school student was over. I would have to change schools. This was not something I could live down. My sister, who had to have been the biggest victim of embarrassment, looked over at me and saw the distress on my face and decided to step in for my sake. She put her hands up to signal the audience to be quiet and yelled, "Hey everyone, stop booing. Let's give a hand to my best friend, Amy. Let's cheer for our real Winter Courts Queen." The crowd started to cheer again and I ran for cover.

Dedication to Kym

Through her own disappointment, my sister saw me in distress and saved me. All day at school, people came up to me and said, "You're lucky you have the sister you do because if you were my sister I would have..." There were many things they said to fill in that blank and none of them were kind. My sister was not mad at me at all. She felt sorry for me and knew it would be hard for me to live through the embarrassment of the day.

Later that year, my parents purchased a page in the back of the yearbook where the family could write a message to their senior graduate. They asked if I wanted to include something. I wrote some of the lyrics to a song by Bette Midler called "Wind beneath My Wings." I mainly chose it for the chorus because it expressed how I felt about my sister. She was my hero who pushed me forward and let me shine.

High school can be tough, but I was not alone. Kym was strong and fearless when I was not. She taught me how to be a bold leader and how to be comfortable in my own skin, never to conform to what everyone else was doing. She had great confidence, and I strived to have it as well. She was a role model for me and looked out for me, even when it meant forsaking herself. She still does that to this day!

Pregnancy and Loss

When I was pregnant with Brady, I called the whole family. Everyone was so excited for us, including Kym, who had two children of her own. What she did not reveal at the time was that she, too, was pregnant. The reason she did not tell us was because she didn't want to take away from my special day, so she waited a few days to make her announcement. Even as an adult, she saw to it that I had my own special moments to shine.

Weeks later, to our heartbreak, Kym lost the child through miscarriage and simultaneously found out she had a rare form of uterine cancer. Since she lived two hours away and I was suffering from major morning sickness, I was unable to be there for her in person the way my heart desired. Kym was so strong through it all. She was very sick from chemo and even lost her hair. I never realized the extent of what she went through because she tried to protect me from her pain and her grief. She did not want me to worry while I was pregnant.

When Brady was born, Kym rushed two hours to be with me. She got there in the nick of time to watch Brady's birth. Delivery should have been difficult for me because about 10 years ago I had broken the first two ribs, by my neck area, and the bones healed wrong. Since then I have lived with chronic neck and back pain. During labor, Kym stood behind me and every time the doctor said push, she lifted me up and pushed me knowing I did not have the neck strength to do it myself. Once again, she was the wind beneath my wings. I had a quick delivery and the doctor said, "You make this look easy." In all seriousness I said, "Is it not supposed to be, because this is really easy." I only realized after that it was easy because my sister was doing all the work.

Kym's Account

Until I asked Kym to write something for this book, she has never been able to open up about her account of the traumatic incident surrounding Ella's birth. Every time I asked her to talk about it, she welled up with tears and said, "I can't talk about it. It's too hard." I know writing this took a lot out of her since it forced her to reflect on one of the worst times of her life. However, I am grateful to her because she is the only person who spent time with Ella during the first few days of Ella's life. She is the only one who had the piece of the puzzle about Ella's early days.

Kym Adair, November 18, 2010

The phone rang about 6:40 a.m. and it was Melanie telling me she was in labor at the hospital. I told her I'd take a shower and drive to Phoenix immediately. I live in Tucson, about two hours away, but I wanted to be there when my sister had her baby. I was in the delivery room when Brady was born and I didn't want to miss my niece's birth. I needed to get there in time to help Melanie. She has a bad neck and back and when Brady was born, it was hard for her to sit up and push; I was there to support her back and neck. I knew she would need my help again. I rushed Melanie off the phone so I could take a shower and get to Phoenix.

By 7:20, I was ready to leave. I had only planned to go for the day and return to my family after the baby was born. As I started my drive, I texted Mel but did not receive a text back from her. About one-and-a-half hours later, I called my mom to find out the hospital location. She did not answer her phone, so I tried Melanie's cell phone. Doug answered. I said hello and asked him how Melanie was doing. He slowly said she was fine and then quickly handed me off to my mom. I received the directions I needed then asked my mom how Melanie was doing. She paused and then said, "She's good. Hurry and come meet the baby." I said, "She had the baby already? Oh, I wanted to be there!" I told my mom I'd be there as soon as possible. I was still about 30 minutes away.

I was so disappointed I missed the birth. When my husband called me about 15 minutes later, I shared my disappointment with him. He asked how far I was from the hospital and I told him I was just a few miles away. He asked me to call him when I arrived. I was confused by this request, but when I got there I called him and told him I was walking into the hospital. I had just entered the elevator when he told me my mom had called him and there was something wrong with Melanie. "What's wrong?" I said. He told me she'd had the baby, but that Melanie was in intensive care. I could tell by his voice he knew more than he was telling me. He said my mom instructed him not to tell me while I was driving because she didn't want me to speed and get into an accident.

As I took this in, the elevator doors opened on the labor and delivery floor. I told him I had to go. I abruptly hung up on him and sprinted toward the labor and delivery area. As I approached, I saw my mom. She was red and crying. She hugged me and as I begged for someone to tell me what happened, she said, "I'm sorry I didn't tell you while you were driving, but I couldn't lose two daughters today." I was confused and shocked. What did she mean "lose two daughters"? What had happened to Melanie?

As my mom guided me into the labor and delivery area, she explained what happened. Almost as quickly as I got there, we were escorted down to the ICU. The hospital staff provided us a private room near Mel's room so we could be close to her.

A few minutes later, Mel was delivered to her room in the ICU and I was able to see her for the first time. I was shocked and traumatized by what I saw. Her body was inflated and swollen; she had tubes coming out of her mouth. Had I not known she was my sister, I would not have guessed it was her. As the doctors attended to her, I left to go see my niece. I had the worst moments of my life over the next hours, but one of the most difficult parts was feeling torn between the joy of seeing Ella and the torment of saying goodbye to my sister. I knew Doug was feeling the same way. Because the medical staff was still evaluating Ella, I could not hold her and that is what I really needed at that moment. I needed to hold a piece of my sister, I needed Ella to know her family was there loving her and that she was not alone. I gazed at her for ten minutes and then went back to Melanie.

Although I knew how serious her condition was and there was a possibility she would not make it, I did not believe it until I touched her for the first time. Her hand was so cold, the way I imagined a corpse to feel. She was totally unresponsive and cold and I broke down in uncontrollable sobs. I sobbed like I had never cried before—a wrenching, heartbreaking cry.

As I finally composed myself, I started talking to her and letting her know I was there. I said, "I love you, and you are strong and can pull through this. I need you in my life."

Throughout the day, I went back and forth between Melanie's room and the nursery. Eventually, it was decided that Melanie would be transported to the new hospital. I wanted to be there with her, but I knew she would want me to stay and take care of her baby. I knew she would not want her sweet, beautiful, brand new baby in a cold, sterile environment. As wonderful as the nurses were, Ella needed the love she deserved from her family after her birth. I also knew Doug needed to stay with Melanie, and in order to do that, he had to know Ella was in good hands.

There was no doubt I was going to stay, but it was not up to me. As I unfolded my plan to Doug, he listened and quietly thanked me. We went back to the nursery so he could hand over the hospital guardianship to me, which allowed me to keep Ella in a private room just as if I had delivered her myself.

She was a beautiful baby. Absolutely perfect! After Mel was transported, my husband, who arrived a few hours earlier, and I were left to take care of Ella. It reminded me of when I had my own baby. My husband, Craig, slept on the couch and I slept in the hospital bed with Ella's bassinet next to me.

She was so tiny. I found myself gazing at her for long periods of time. For the first few hours that evening, it was apparent she was not eating a lot of formula. The nurse changed the nipple, and from that moment on Ella ate like a champ. She was a great baby. She ate and then fell right back to sleep. Throughout the night, I stared at her and I felt guilty because my sister should have been there experiencing this joy and instead, I was.

At about 3:00 a.m. the nurse came in to check on us. I asked her, "Can Ella go home tomorrow?" She said that Ella would probably need to stay another 24 hours. She explained to me that because Ella had a traumatic entry into the world, the staff wanted to monitor her a little longer. When she said Ella had a traumatic entry, I assumed she was referring to what happened to Melanie and the need for an emergency C-Section. She asked me if I knew about the delivery, and I said I did not. She proceeded to explain to me that when Ella was born, she was not breathing. The doctors immediately started CPR and chest compressions. For three minutes she did not breathe. The nurse said finally she took a gasping breath of air and never stopped breathing again. The medical team was relieved and grateful they had saved her because they did not know if her mother would survive.

The next morning, my mom arrived at the hospital early so my husband and I could go visit Mel. She stayed with Ella until I returned.

When Craig and I arrived, it was apparent that a lot of people had followed Melanie to the new hospital. Along with the people, who clearly had just awakened, there was an enormous amount of food in the waiting room that Mel's friends had commandeered. I found Doug and hugged him. He was disheveled and looked exhausted. We talked for a while and I told him about my night with Ella. I shared with him what the nurse had told me about Ella's birth. He had not been aware of the details.

Eventually, Doug was told that the medical staff was taking Melanie back to surgery to remove the packing they had left in her open abdomen and to close her. They asked Doug if he would like to go see her before she went to surgery. He invited me to come along with him.

As we approached her room, I could see she had color back in her face and when I touched her hand, it was warm again. The most amazing feeling rushed over me. It was hope. The doctors informed us they had reduced her sedatives because they wanted to see if she would respond to them. They would be able to get their first indication whether there was any brain injury caused by her lack of oxygen.

Doug started talking to Melanie and for the first time her eyes had life in them. They were not glazed over; instead, there was a faint light in them. Doug looked at me in amazement. I stroked her arm as I told her I was there. I told her I had been taking care of baby Ella. As Doug and I spoke about Ella, something clicked for Melanie, and she tried to move her arms and sit up. The nurse asked me if I had a photo of Ella. I ran into the lobby and grabbed a phone with a photo of Ella on it and rushed with it back into her room. As soon as she saw the photo of her precious baby, she was determined to get out of the bed. She started moving around again and when she tried to pull out the tubes in her mouth, the nurses restrained her more. The nurses told us they had to give her sedatives to calm her down and that it was time for surgery.

We kissed her goodbye and walked into the hall. We just held on to each other and cried. It was hard to see her so upset and frustrated, but it was the most wonderful thing in the world to see her moving, hearing, and understanding that Ella had been born. As we exited the intensive care unit and entered the waiting room, we were able to give the good news to everyone. It was an amazing moment. It was a miracle.

I had the privilege of staying with Ella for the next two nights, one in the hospital and one at Melanie and Doug's home. Ella was finally able to meet her mom 48 hours after her birth. I will forever treasure the time I had with Ella during her first hours of life. It was a blessing I will never forget and she will always be in my heart.

My Sister Stayed Behind

It is no surprise that when the nurse asked for someone to stay behind and take care of Ella, Kym would be the one to volunteer. She stayed and protected Gabriella and loved her like she has always done for me.

The Lord provided for me and Doug to send my sister to care for Ella, but he also gave my sister a great gift in this tragedy. As I mentioned earlier, Kym not only suffered the loss of a child through miscarriage, but also lost her chance ever to have children again because of the kind of cancer she had. Kym was given the unique experience of being with Ella, taking on the motherly role with a newborn, and it gave Ella and Kym a bond that can never be broken.

My greatest sadness in all of this is the fact that I could not be there for my own daughter. I was not the first to see her face, hear the sound of her cry, or hold her for the first time and make her feel my love. I will be eternally grateful to my sister for stepping in to ensure that my baby girl, her niece, felt the kind of love she deserved. Kym has always been the wind beneath my wings and continues to be the wind beneath Ella's wings, too!

Chapter Nine

BROKEN "HARTS" AND MY SON

*B*ecause everything happened so fast during the emergency C-section and the CPR, my anesthesiologist was unable to give me any pain medication during the procedure. Basically, the surgeons cut me open without any form of numbing agent because I was dead and there was no time. My anesthesiologist feared that if I did regain consciousness, I might remember the pain of being cut open, so he gave me a medication that would erase my memory.

Many have asked me if I saw "the light" during my death. If there was a glorious, shining light to Jesus, I am sure I followed it, but unfortunately, I have no memory of it. As much as I would like the memory, the truth is, I do not need it because I know what the light looks like. I have followed "the light" since high school.

Transformation

My mother dropped me off at the entrance of a church hall around midnight the summer before my sophomore year in high school. She was forcing me to go on a church youth group trip to California. I was mad! I walked in the hall to find a bunch of faces I did not know. I hated making new friends, especially when I liked the ones I already had. People all of a sudden started to call my name and when I looked over at them, I discovered they were not looking at me. Then I noticed where they were looking: at a blonde, beautiful, bubbly girl who was obviously very popular with this group, and of all names she could have, her name was "Melanie." She had *my* name. This angered me even more.

I got on the bus, put on my headphones, and just wanted to fall asleep and pretend not to be on this trip. The only consolation was a really attractive guy sitting in the seat across from me. It gave me hope that maybe this would not be the worst trip of my life.

Later, I felt a tap on my shoulder, and thinking it might the cute guy, I opened my eyes, only to find Melanie looking at me. She was sitting behind me and had reached around the seat to greet me and shake my hand. It was then she discovered we shared the same name. She thought it was a great thing, whereas I still preferred being unique. As much as I did not want to like this girl, there was just something about her. She had this joy—a joy I did not see in my friends at school.

As she talked about God, all I could think was that I wanted to hear more. It was obvious she had something about her I wanted—something I desired but had not known was out there. After much talking, we fell asleep and woke up in sunny California.

The first day there, we went to the beach, where we met up with a bunch of other churches from Arizona, California, and New Mexico. The cute guy befriended me and I spent the day hanging out with him, my new friend, Melanie, and a bunch of other teens. The cute guy had a name…it was Mark Hart and he, too, had this light about him. He was not like guys I knew. He was passionate about the Lord and was not afraid to show it. Normally this would not seem cool to me, but he had a really engaging way of talking about faith.

At the end of the day, we celebrated Mass on the beach with over a thousand other teens. I use the word "celebrated" on purpose. This was not the typical Mass that I was used to. No. The music was loud and people were singing their praises to God and lifting their arms to the sky as if they were reaching up for their fathers. I thought, "What is going on? Young people don't act like this." But their love for God was tattooed on their faces and sewn in their hearts. They were not embarrassed or afraid to show their faith. I looked around at their faces and tears began to fall from my eyes. I was crying. Me, the strongest, most unemotional person on earth was crying. Sobbing like a baby, tears of complete joy poured down my face and for the first time in my whole life, I felt God's presence in my heart. The word "faith" had a whole new meaning to me. I finally had a real feeling to go along with all the knowledge I learned about Catholicism in grade school. This was the beginning of my faith journey, the start of my transformation.

After I returned home, everything changed. My life was turned upside down. I lost friends at school, gained more at church, and became totally head over heels for this amazing man.

The Light

When we got off the bus in Phoenix, Mark asked me to go to adoration, which was what the teens did for their Monday night prayer group. I did not even know what adoration was; all I knew was that Mark was cute, so I would go. At Saint Maria Goretti Church, adoration was in a beautiful glass chapel separate from the church with a very large monstrance in the middle with kneelers and statues of angels surrounding it. People knelt when they came in, so I did, too. I took my seat by Mark. I am not sure I really knew what was going on there because I was just interested in making a good impression on Mark. He explained to me that Jesus was in the monstrance, but I was more interested in him than Jesus.

Mark invited me to prayer group the next week, so of course I went. But this time, I went in by myself and sat in silence and looked at this monstrance where Jesus was. Mark came in and I have to admit that this time my attention was split between Mark and Jesus. Mark invited me again to come the next week. Of course I went; but this time when I sat in that chapel, I did not notice Mark. All I saw was Jesus. I could not take my eyes off him. Something was happening in my heart. I was falling in love.

Mark left for college in Indiana the next week, so I went to adoration on my own. Something was pulling me there. I went every week for the next three years. But that was not enough for me. I had to see this man I fell in love with and developed a personal relationship with so I ended up stopping by that chapel almost every day for years. That ended up not being enough for me either, so I began going to Mass every day. This was true love. I loved Jesus and I knew he loved me, everything about me. It was in that chapel where I also became close to his mother, Mary. It was there I would go and imagine myself resting in her arms, asking her to show me the road of a true woman of God since she was the perfect example.

My Life-Long Friends

Melanie and Mark are still two of my best friends. They led me to the light—the light of Christ. They showed me the way when we were teenagers and they have shown me the way ever since. Had I paid attention on that California trip, I would have recognized Mark already had his eyes on another Melanie. Later in life, Melanie and Mark married and now they have three beautiful girls, for one of whom I am the godmother. The Hart family is like family to us, and Melanie is part of that team of women I want Ella to have as examples. The only reason I did not ask her to be in the delivery room, too, was because I needed a trusted friend to take care of my most precious son while Doug and I were at the hospital.

Where Was My Son?

It gave me great comfort to read Kym's account and learn more about where Ella was and what she was doing while I was unresponsive to life. Next in my quest to connect the pieces, I wanted to know what Brady was doing during this time. I knew he had gone to stay with Melanie and Mark, but did he know what was happening? Was he sad to be without us? Was he okay? How were two of my very best friends in the world able to cope with taking care of him while mourning me? As a mother I had to know, so I asked Melanie to give me their account.

Melanie's Account

When I coded, Brady had just been taken out of the room, but when he returned and I was gone, he began asking about me, saying, "Mommy, where's mommy?" Brooke tried to distract him by letting him open a gift and then Meghan took him to the play area, where she played with him while fighting back tears. He kept asking Meg, "Why are you sad?" Meg said to him, "Your mommy is sick and very tired. She needs to get better." Brady kept repeating, "Mommy is sick. Mommy is sick," not really understanding the gravity of what was happening.

Doug immediately called Melanie and Mark and asked them to come to the hospital and pick up Brady so he would not figure out anything more. They had the incredibly hard job of entertaining my child and making sure he was happy, while their hearts were breaking for what was happening to me, their friend of 20 years. The following is Melanie and Mark's account about what their family endured the first 24 hours of my trauma. Melanie wrote it on behalf of the two of them.

Melanie Hart, November 29, 2010

The morning began so joyfully. Melanie waited until 6:00 a.m. before calling our house. Her early morning text messages had gone unanswered, with my cell in the other room. Of course, having little ones of my own, it would take an explosion to wake me out of my sleep…but that, of course, is part of the joy of children!

I received a call around 8:40 a.m. from Doug. I asked how everything was going. In a broken voice, Doug could only offer, "Something went wrong. Melanie's heart stopped during labor. She's in critical condition." Crying, he frantically told me of the events that had just taken place. They had rushed my best friend off to the O.R., trying to resuscitate her. "They think she had an embolism. Can you come get Brady right now?"

I immediately began to cry. I could hear the fear and the concern in Doug's voice. Beside myself, I gathered my three daughters quickly into the car, trying to hold it together. Then I received a text telling me that Melanie had coded for the second time. As we drove, I asked my little girls to pray. Though they did not fully understand what was transpiring, seeing the tears in my eyes and the pain in my voice, they quickly stopped fighting over dolls and began saying "Hail Marys" for Melanie and her baby girl.

I repeatedly dialed my husband's cell, knowing he was at Mass but hoping his phone was on vibrate. A few minutes later, he called me back and immediately left to meet me at the hospital.

I rushed into the hospital not knowing what to expect. Meghan and Brooke met me at the doorway, and broke down in tears. Our old friend, the newly ordained Father John Parks arrived almost simultaneously, bringing the Church's healing presence with him. As I entered the labor room, I saw that the family was visibly—and understandably—in a state of shock and disbelief. My heart wrenched inside of me looking at Doug. Wanting to get Brady removed from such a stressful and painful setting as soon as possible, we headed down to the parking lot to gather his car seat and toys. Our hope was to change Brady's focus and to give Doug a brief relief from parenting so his full attention could go to his dying bride.

The exchange in the parking lot was brief, but impactful. Words failed to express what we all feared and were feeling. I am sure Brady was very confused but, luckily, he had several little girls to take his attention and to treat him like a rock star.

The next several hours are still a blur. Phone calls and text messages came in a flurry not only from Doug and the rest of the family, but from around the world. Our home phone, cell phones, e-mails, Facebook pages, and Twitter feeds were flooded by countless souls— from childhood friends to total strangers— around the globe looking for information, and sending out prayer requests for Melanie and little Ella. Thousands fell on their knees simultaneously. Thousands more forwarded prayer requests on their own blogs and pages.

It amazes me that as Doug was told to say goodbye to his wife, he still managed to call us regularly to check in on Brady and keep us informed about Melanie's condition, setbacks, and progress.

The afternoon was gut-wrenching. As the correspondence flooded in, Mark and I struggled to keep a joyful mood in the home (for Brady and the girls) all while we were fielding phone calls and wondering if the beautiful two-year-old boy we held would ever see his mother again. Would he remember her? Would she walk with him on his road of life or just become a story of inspiration? I was so thankful to have my husband and family to help play with him since just looking into his eyes that afternoon filled me with such fear and pain.

As the calls continued and the outlook grew increasingly dim, my mother and sister dropped everything to drive down to our house to help and offer support. I remained steadily on the phone with Doug and Meghan to get reports, while Kemi (who had arrived at the hospital) kept Mark updated.

As the sun set on this horrible day, they told us Melanie's critical condition was worsening and they were preparing to move her to a new hospital. We made dinner, prepared an extra bed, and prayed like we never had before. As we put Brady to bed, his exhausted little body finally fell asleep. Mark and I prayed for him fervently and sat, tears streaming down our faces, trusting in God's will but hoping he would work a miracle of healing and that Brady would be held by his mother once again.

By the grace of God, Brady, who normally did not sleep through the night, slept for almost 12 hours. We did not. Mark and I were up throughout the night, tossing and turning, fearing any moment would bring a call bearing terrible news.

As the sun rose, we received more news from Doug and were overjoyed to hear Melanie had not only made it through the night but—miraculously—had begun to show some improvement.

All of a sudden, things began to change. "When can I see my Daddy and Mommy? Is she still resting?" little Brady inquired with beautiful innocence.

"Very soon" we replied, hoping and praying the Holy Spirit would not leave us liars.

Later that morning Doug called again to tell us more about Melanie's miraculous progress and his deep desire to see Brady as soon as possible.

We spent the afternoon in the waiting room with Melanie's entire family and close friends. Seeing the relief and joy in Doug's eyes and upon the faces of Melanie's family as Brady got out of the elevator (and took over the floor) was a gift. His energetic presence lifted the cloud of anxiety even further.

Though we did not get to see Melanie that day, we were there as the good news and positive prognosis was announced. She was progressing at an incredible rate when we left the hospital and brought Brady back to the princess castle with us for another night, allowing Doug to stay with Melanie in her intensive care room. Enlivened from his hospital visit, Brady was decidedly more combative on the second night of his stay. We took it as a good sign that he was comfortable enough to fight with his female counterparts over every last toy. Again, though, he drifted off to sleep—this time under decidedly different conditions—and Mark and I fell on our knees in grateful awe at how the Lord had moved in a 24-hour time span.

The next day brought another visit to the hospital. I was able to see Melanie this time, to sit at her bedside, and to look in her eyes. She was far from herself. I was not sure if she really knew who I was or why I was there. It was a challenging moment. I was thankful for her miraculous recovery but worried I might never get "the old Melanie" back again. I was filled with so many emotions. As I saw and held Ella for the first time and spoke to my dear friend, though, I was overwhelmed by God's goodness. Somehow, in the midst of chaos, it was a very peaceful moment. Ella was absolutely perfect and Melanie, literally back from the dead, showed the same strength and resilience I have come to expect from her over almost 20 years of friendship.

Looking back at the entire experience with Melanie, I am beginning to see how deeply this has affected my own motherhood. It is impossible to go through something like this and not realize how we took for granted how "easily" most deliveries go. I ask myself and the Lord why she went through this whole ordeal. I reflect on what I am supposed to take from it, not only as a mother, but also as a child of God. It has reminded me of how beautiful and fragile life is—a life we cannot control no matter how hard we try. God has a plan for each of us (Jer. 29:11) and he absolutely hears our prayers (Jer. 29:12). We have to trust that no matter what he wills or allows us to go through will ultimately draw us closer to him (Prov. 3:5–6; James 1:2), even in the most tragic and devastating of situations (Is. 41:10). This whole journey has reminded me again that God is bigger. God is bigger than our humanity, our own understanding, and our own plans. His love was present regardless of the outcome, but his mercy revealed, again, how small we are and how great he is.

During Melanie's recovery at home, I visited once a week to offer maternal support, but more importantly love, as she slowly got back to full strength. I could tell she was healing physically, but spiritually she had been made anew. God had great plans for Melanie and her family from the beginning—to unleash a greatness within her that had not yet been seen. She was lighter now…softer…more open…in short, freer. The "conquer the world" Melanie was not gone, but had given way to a gentler Mel—more present to life and its fragility. In the midst of all the stress and turmoil, her faith had only grown. She had faced and—by the grace

of God—survived death, literally. As wonderful a woman of
God as she had been before, the new Melanie surpassed even
her own example of God's goodness.

As odd as it sounds, I am immeasurably thankful for
where this experience took her and us. Our faith deepened,
our friendship strengthened, our prayer life grew. And our
appreciation for the gifts of life, family, and friends will
never be the same. Who would have dreamed that Melanie
dying on that Wednesday morning in July would help us
all—including her—to live so much more fully? God did.

Lights of Christ

Melanie and Mark have always been the light of Christ
for me and to know they were the light of Christ to Brady
during all this is a great comfort to me as a mother. In the
last paragraph of Melanie's account she expressed what many
have in the months following my return—God worked
through this tragedy and suffering to provide hope, healing,
and an increase of faith for many of us involved in it.

Chapter Ten
LIVING EULOGIES

*W*henever I went to funerals in my younger years, I wondered who would show up to mine. Would only the first two rows be taken up or would it be standing room only? This may sound creepy, but I feel as though I have had the opportunity to be a fly on the wall at my own funeral. In the hospital and upon returning home, I had things expressed to me that usually are only heard when someone dies. Someday I will look back at my survival of an amniotic fluid embolism and it will probably seem like a short bit of time in my life, but I will always remember the complete, raw, exposed, and honest feelings people expressed. I know many did it because they thought it might be their last opportunity to tell me, but no matter the reason, I will never be the same. Their love is overflowing in me. One person in particular who shared feelings I never knew she had for me was my sister Kari.

Kari's Account and Honest Feelings

My sister Kari and I are ten years apart and have different personalities and ways of doing things, but I always know that if I am ever in need, Kari will drop everything to be by my side. There have been stretches in our lives where we leaned on each other immensely and then other times when we grew apart. Regardless of where we are in our relationship or busy lives, we have a great love for one another, but not one we ever really verbalized.

Kari sat down just two days after the trauma and wrote down her thoughts. Her account is very special because she wrote it when her emotions were fresh. I do not receive compliments well and when people do compliment me, I try to deflect to somebody else or something else or I just become sarcastic so they will stop. Including this account from my sister is really hard for me because it forces me to really receive her words of affirmation and love. Many of Kari's words have grabbed hold of my heart and caused me to pause. Some of what she reveals are feelings and thoughts I did not know she had for me. Reading them chokes me up; it's like I'm reading a living eulogy and seeing into her real thoughts and feelings. This is an incredible gift. Her words will be etched in my heart forever!

Kari Holt, July 30, 2010

I do not really know how to put into words what I want to say about the miracle (I should say miracles) I have witnessed in just a 48-hour period, but I really want to share with everyone the miraculous and inspiring event, so I will do my best. This will probably be really raw; however, it will be the simple truth of each and every one of my emotions and my witness of what makes this story so inspirational.

I am just the average person living in this world trying to get by and doing my best to play by all the rules. I am a single mom of three boys, Brandon, 11, Evan, 10, and Keean, 7. I am blessed in so many ways and I have an abundance of faith in God.

My sister Mel…Wow! It is really hard for me to put into words how beautiful this woman is because she is so beyond beautiful in every single way imaginable. Melanie is 10 years younger than me, so I do not really remember too much about growing up together, but I do remember when she was born (she cried A LOT).

She always had a really pure way about her. As a youth she never followed the crowd, but she wanted to fit in, just not the way most girls go about being accepted. She liked boys, really cute boys, but never had a long-term boyfriend because boys wanted more than she was willing to give… if you know what I mean! Honestly, our family really wondered if Mel would ever get married because she had such high standards.

Mel went off to college and although I do not know much about her experiences there as I lived out of state at the time, I do know she wanted to be a teacher. I desperately tried talking her out of it because teaching has long hours with little pay. She did not care about the pay. She cared about changing lives.

She graduated and got a teaching job at a local Scottsdale high school, but after just 4 years of feeling boxed in, she said enough is enough. She realized that in that environment she could not make the kind of difference she wanted to make.

At this point in my life, I was married and had my first son, Brandon, and as young as Melanie was, she totally stepped up and wanted to be there with my child all the time to love, kiss, and care for him. Come on, what 22-year-old wants to spend time with family that way?? Yep, you guessed it, Melanie. Then I had Evan, and, oh boy! was Melanie there for my little Evan, too. And then Keean… holy cow! She was so excited to babysit all three at every opportunity. Who does this with such love and sincerity at that age?? Oh yeah, you guessed it again…Melanie.

Even with the age difference between us, my little sister had so much more of a way about her. Boy, I sure envied that about her. She used to talk about how she was going to have all these children and how she was going to raise them. And all I would do is laugh and tell her, "Just wait, sis, because you can say and think all of that now, but once you have babies, they are born with their own personality, and no matter how great a parent you are and the manners you teach them, it kind of goes out the door during certain periods."

Yet there was this thing about her that was so inspirational and that words cannot describe. I was in my thirties with tons of life experiences, kids, etc., and I had my little sis talking to me in a way that made me feel guilty because she was so pure and Godlike, but without any of the typical in-your-face preaching. Melanie has this way about her that I think everyone who meets her envies her in some way. To watch Mel and the way she is in life is something indescribable.

As we got older, the truth of the matter is, as much as I love, I mean LOVE, my sister, she and I have not always seen eye-to-eye. I just grew up differently than she did, in a different era and different circumstances. I was more of a rebel and she was not; however, as many differences and arguments as we've had…created mostly by me…she has ALWAYS forgiven me. There were times she probably felt she didn't know how to get along with me, but she always was the better person and told me she loved me and forgave me. Can you believe it? I am the adult. Is that not my responsibility to the younger sibling?

Melanie is a second mother to my boys. Again, I cannot explain in words how incredible she is because even with all the things going on in her life, she is always there for me and my boys —let me say ALWAYS again—and she has never, ever complained once about what her day was like or what she needed to do. She just zipped her lips. Are you starting to see why I'm writing this? Just wait.

Long story short, Melanie started a Christian T-shirt company called Refuge Clothing Co. and sold shirts to many Christians who wanted to be hip yet faithful to the good Lord above. She also worked for a local nonprofit pro-life organization where she touched many lives and saved many babies. Now she travels the United States and talks to young people about chastity, staying pure, respecting one's body and self, being modest, and loving God.

I have an abundance of faith in the good Lord above, my boys and I go to church every single Sunday, my kids are involved in serving, they are in the youth program, and I am in a women's group. My boys and I know that without God and faith in him, we are nothing. But that is still not one single ounce of the life Melanie lives. My little sister is bigger, brighter, smarter, and holier than I can ever be.

Two days ago, Melanie text-messaged me on July 28, 2010, at 4:27 a.m., and said, "I'm @ hospital. 4 dilated. Contractions every 3 to 5. They r admitting me. Not in actual room yet. May b a while." At 6:21 a.m. she called my cell phone, and I answered, "Did you have your baby?" and she said, "No, but I'm five centimeters, got the epidural, and the nurse said I should deliver by noon. I love you and please pray for us." Her excitement and unbelievable happiness made me so happy for her that I prayed for her and her baby and family the second I hung up.

At 8:13 a.m. I received a phone call from our mom. All I heard was, "She coded, she coded." I was trying to say what, who, but just said, "I'm coming." I had no idea what happened. One minute my bubbly can't-wait-to-be-a-mother sister was calling me with excitement, and the next I heard the voice of our mother in complete despair.

I jumped up, got dressed, screamed at my kids to wake up and get dressed. I told them, "I think Aunt Melanie died. Get dressed and let's go." My kids were frantic, I was frantic, the place was a mess as we tried to get out the door, and we did not know what was going on. We just knew it was bad!

We got to the hospital and learned that our precious Melanie, the happy-go-lucky woman who wants to be a mother to six children or more, lover to her husband and child, supporter of all her family and friends, speaker to the

nation about pro-life issues, savior to so many in need, and
so much more I cannot even tell you, had just gone into
cardiac arrest. What? Cardiac arrest? What? How does a
33-year-old go into cardiac arrest?

When I arrived, my family explained what had already
happened, and we all sat and waited anxiously to find out
more. Doctors were bringing us one piece of bad news after
another, and all of us were just bawling and saying, "This
can't be happening." Friends gathered in prayer and said the
Rosary and called all their friends and family members to
pray, pray, pray. Every minute there was a story of how this
church in this city was praying for her and/or having a vigil
that evening to pray for her. People were literally coming
out of the woodwork to pray for her, even if they didn't
know her.

When the positive news came in regarding Melanie's
second surgery, we fell to our knees and said, "Thank God!"
and hugged and kissed and cried tears of joy. We knew she
was very critical and not out of the woods, but it was a
miracle she was still alive.

Amidst the glimpses of hope, bad news continued to
trickle in; it seemed like anything that can go wrong with a
person was going wrong with Melanie. I thought, "There is
no way, God. Please don't take her! Her baby needs to know
her mama, her son needs his mama, and her husband needs
his wife! I don't understand God. I think there are more
people on earth that need her more than you need her now.
Please, God, don't take her, please, please, please!"

When we packed up and headed over to the new
hospital, we heard an enormous amount of stories of
prayers for Melanie, including that she was the number
one Googled person in Arizona for the day and was in the
top 100 on Twitter, and eventually in the top 10. Articles
in different states were being written about her, the bishop
of Phoenix asked for prayers for Melanie, and so on. Can
you believe this? I knew Melanie had touched many lives

and had many friends, but this was just amazing. Who gets this kind of response? Literally, thousands and thousands of people were praying for one woman and this was all taking place within a 15-hour period. "Wow," I thought, "How blessed are we to have this for our Melanie?"

My Sister's Overwhelming Words

I cannot help but be completely overwhelmed by my sister's love for me. Kari is a tough cookie and has persevered through a lot in her life. When I was in the fifth grade, my mother went to the holy land of Medjugorie and had an incredible conversion. I remember her coming back and taking every picture off the wall and putting up Jesus. It was a little shocking and confusing for us kids. We were Catholic and went to church on Sundays, but we were not used to the level of faith my mother brought home with her. To put it into words, she became a devout Catholic, living and breathing the faith. Because I was the youngest, my mother shaped my faith. She is the reason why I can say I had a solid Catholic upbringing. My two oldest siblings were grown up and Kari was already out of the house by then, so she never got the level of faith-filled upbringing I did. She was Catholic, but did not practice for many years. It was my great prayer for my sister to come back to the Church. While my faith journey was somewhat easy and handed to me, Kari had to search for it and really commit on her own to living a life pleasing to the Lord. At age twenty-two, she did have a conversion of heart. It has been a privilege to witness her return to the faith and watch her boys become so involved in church.

When I read her account and found out my nephews were at the hospital, I could only imagine the pain they, too, were feeling as they witnessed this day. As much as I wish they never had to go through that terrifying day, I am pleased to know they witnessed a miracle and they were able to see how powerful prayer is. I hope this experience gives them a faith that can move mountains!

Chapter Eleven
The Prayer Chain Begins

*M*iracles happen. Never did I expect them to happen to me. Never did I expect people from around the world to pray for me. Never did I expect people would stop what they were doing to write articles about me. Never did I expect people would walk out of their jobs, step away from their families, and hop on planes to be in a waiting room to hold a vigil for me. Never did I expect the social mediums that often seem like lawless vehicles for people to do what they want instead of what they ought would be used to ignite a powerful chain of prayers. Never did I expect conferences would stop to pray for me or radio stations to air updates about me, for priests to say homilies and hold prayer services, nor the bishop I respect beyond measure to send out a message for everyone to pray for me. Who deserves this sort of response? Surely not me.

I am humbled. I honestly do not know what I have done to deserve all that people have done for me. It is overwhelming to think about it. When I was in the hospital, the stories of all these things were shared with me. I definitely could not comprehend them in the state I was in, but coming home and absorbing them has been an incredibly humbling experience.

Like Sisters

Brooke and Meghan are blood-related sisters who are like little sisters to me; they have been a part of my life for many years. They are both incredible, young women who I admire and love dearly. They were in the room when I coded. I had invited them to see the incredible birth of my child; but instead, they watched me die in front of their eyes. Even though they were traumatized by what they witnessed, they set the wheels in motion for people to pray. They began calling any and everyone they knew, pleading for prayers, which started the great prayer chain. The first people Brooke called were the Poor Clare nuns to ask them to pray. Meghan, too, texted everyone she knew and the domino effect of prayer began.

While at the hospital, Brooke and Meghan shared with me that constant prayer was the only thing that gave everyone in the waiting room hope and comfort during the incident, but there were times where the group felt completely hopeless. They told me that at a certain point everyone was volunteering to organize meals for Doug. They said that each person discussed who would take which days to help Doug watch the kids while he was at work and who would come in the evenings to help put them to bed. They spoke about me as if I were dead, but that was the gravity of the situation. All they could do was plan for the worst and pray for a miracle. These two sisters told me that they spent all day and all night praying rosaries, divine chaplets, and even attending Mass on my behalf.

Men Like Brothers

In addition to these two sisters, two men who are like brothers to me, came to the hospital to pray for me and led others to pray. Father Muir and Father Parks have inspired me to be holier, to be smarter in my faith, and they challenged me to be a better person. When Father Muir was a deacon, he presided over my wedding vows. As a priest, he and Father Parks administered the Anointing of the Sick while I was in critical condition. Father Parks is Brady's godfather and he baptized Ella.

When word about my critical condition reached them, they both came to be by my bedside to offer their priestly services as well as to pray. I had included Father Parks in the text I sent many of my friends about amazing epidurals. At 8:39 a.m., he received a text from Brooke that said, "Melanie has coded and is in critical condition. She needs prayers." Father Parks told me he freaked out a little and immediately told the church where he works that he was leaving to administer an Anointing of the Sick. He also contacted the Poor Clare nuns in Arizona to ask them to storm heaven with prayers. They continued the prayer chain by contacting the Poor Clare nuns in Alabama and asking them to pray, too. These cloistered nuns have perpetual adoration every day, which means at every hour a nun is assigned to pray and adore Jesus in the Blessed Sacrament. One of the nuns in Alabama posted a picture of Gabriella and put a note on the door of the chapel requesting prayers for us. Every nun that came to pray would pray for us every hour of the day. In addition, Father Parks contacted all of his priest friends and asked them to make my situation their Mass intention. He said that over those first two days, I may have had at least 10 Masses said for me just in Arizona. When he shared these details, he exclaimed, "That's an insane amount of grace."

Father Muir was actually at the Poor Clares' monastery just outside of town when I coded. Upon receiving Brooke's

frantic plea for prayers, the nuns informed him of my
sudden death. He could not believe it. He said that on his
drive to the hospital he began calling friends and family
trying to get updates.

Bringing the Spirit of the Priesthood

Eventually Father Muir met up with Father Parks at the
hospital. When he got there, he went to my ICU room after
my severed artery had been repaired. He told me that when
he first saw me, it looked like I had an inflatable raft on top
of me, and he barely recognized me. He told me it was so
sad to see me that way. He decided I had plenty of friends in
the waiting room and what I needed most was for him to be
my priest, so our friendship became secondary as the spirit
of the priesthood took over.

Father Muir spoke with Doug, who was visibly still
in shock. Doug said to him, "Today they told me to say
goodbye to my wife. I do not ever want to hear them say
that again." This is when he knew how serious it was. He
had a sense of awe at the mystery and grace of our marriage
as he had a flashback to our wedding. He thought to
himself, "God knew this would happen the day Mel and
Doug got married. When Doug said, "I do," he was saying
"I do" to this day even though he did not know it yet, and it
is amazing to see how strong his love is." He then recognized
this was the grace of the sacrament of marriage. Father Muir
and Father Parks then administered the sacrament of the
Anointing of the Sick.

Adoration Prayer Services

Father Parks and musician Matt Maher held a prayer
service for me when it was thought I would not survive.

Many people who attended the service said it was an incredible gift to gather with a community of people and pray. They said their sadness was turned into trust—God was in charge and they could have peace in knowing he would take care of things.

Father Parks and Matt are my friends, so I know they must have been hurting for me and for what Doug was going through; but still, they put their pain aside and led people in prayer and musical worship. As they shared their talents through their own heartache, others were led to hope, to find solace in prayer, and to trust in the greatness of the Lord. Words can never express my gratitude for their ability to comfort those who showed up that night. Father Parks mentioned afterward there was a real sense of hope and consolation. The evening was not planned out at all, but ended up perfectly planned. Father Parks even stayed to offer confessions for about an hour and a half.

Father Muir also held Eucharistic Adoration at a church in North Scottsdale. When he went into the chapel, he was exhausted since his morning started so early with his travel to the Poor Clares. He was emotionally and physically drained, but during this holy hour, not only were others able to sit silently in front of the Lord, but the Lord gave Father Muir a renewed energy and strength that allowed him to return to the hospital to see me again. This truly uplifted all who were still there, including my husband.

Chapter Twelve
STORMING HEAVEN

Not only did Brooke, Meghan, and my priest friends solicit prayers for me, but so did many others once they caught word of what was transpiring. Two of those friends dispersed their request for prayers by writing articles they posted on the Internet, where they were read by thousands across the world. I am grateful to Chris Faddis and Mark Henry for knowing me enough to write such beautiful pieces and to realize I would welcome the idea of people praying for me.

I know when I hear of people's suffering and struggles, I often pause to ask myself if they would want me to share them with others because so many people are private. But when it comes to people coming to our rescue in prayer, we cannot be prideful or private. We have to allow them to reach outside of themselves, even for us.

I am glad I did not have the opportunity to give permission for these articles to go out because I might have been prideful myself, not wanting people to worry about me or know my pain. I am grateful my friends were led by the Spirit. They had the courage to share my story because they wanted what was best for me…for people to pray and to know of the great miracle taking place. I often say my survival is a great miracle, but really, the greatest miracle is all the people who prayed.

The articles gave people a picture of who they were praying for and an easy outlet to forward them on to other friends. The first article, "Urgent Prayer Request: Melanie Pritchard in Critical Condition" was posted on July 28, 2010, by Chris Faddis, friend and publisher of *www. livinggracefully.net*. On the left-hand side of the article was a picture of me, followed by information about the critical circumstances I faced during labor and in the hours that followed. In his plea for prayers, he gave readers insight into my life so they would know who exactly was in need of prayer. He requested that people pray to the late Pope John Paul II. He said:

> I am personally begging you to get on your knees and pray for Melanie and her family. Chastity speaker and friend, Mary Beth Bonnacci, offered this suggestion today, "My friend Julie Alexander, also a passionate defender of life, came back from a should-have-been-fatal heart emergency through the intercession of John Paul II. I am going to start praying for his intercession!"
>
> It is fitting. Melanie, who has been so inspired and guided by John Paul II's teachings and writings, deserves his intercession and prayers. So I ask you to pray and continue praying, asking venerable John Paul the Great to pray for Melanie and to intercede on her behalf. I am hoping and praying this Living Gracefully community will come together in sincere prayer for this holy woman of God and for her wonderful husband, Doug, and their children. We are hoping and praying for a miracle and ultimately asking God's grace in this situation.[2]

Chris's article on the information highway sparked many people to pray.

More Than He Could Have Imagined

We have been friends with Chris's family for many years, and Doug and I are the godparents to his oldest child. So a few months after the incident, I spoke with Chris about what prompted him to write the article. He said when he had heard how extreme things were and that I was probably going to die, he felt called to send out the urgent prayer request. He intended for it to be read by people associated with his website, but what happened was more than he could have ever imagined.

He posted the article in the evening, and by morning, 10,000 people had already viewed it. In addition, other popular websites picked it up and posted it. Chris informed me that 2,400 people posted the article's link on their Facebook pages, so the actual number of people who were exposed to it was well over 150,000. He said his webpage received so much traffic he had to pay extra to increase the bandwidth that night!

Real-Time Updates

In addition to writing the article, Chris regularly updated his website with real-time information about facts he was learning along with those from the people present at the hospital. The comments included on the website were extremely valuable to me when I began piecing together what had happened. These updates helped me connect more pieces of the puzzle since they include the actual times of the events.

> 11:30 p.m. (AZ time) 7/28/10—Kemi Ndolo (bass player of the Matt Maher Band and childhood friend of Doug) posted: "Just left the hospital, Melanie is doing better. Still

needs lots and lots of prayers. Gabriella is gorgeous and healthy. Doug is staying strong and positive."

9:42 a.m. (AZ time) 7/29/10—Mark Hart, vice-president of LIFE TEEN and long time friend of Melanie's posted to Twitter: "Melanie was stable through the night. She's heading back into surgery soon. Keep the prayers coming, please!"

10:07 a.m. (AZ Time) 7/29/10—Word is that Melanie was weaned off of sedation this morning to see how "neurologically intact" she was and woke up and began reaching for Doug and crying. She was trying to get out of bed. Her lungs and heart have improved, and she is now headed in for another surgery. GOD IS GOOD! Keep those prayers coming as she is not out of the water, yet. This is the first major sign of improvement.—Chris

1 p.m. (AZ Time) 7/29/10—Brooke Burns, long time friend of Mel's and her collaborator at the Foundation for Life and Love, posted this great news on Facebook: "I just want to pass along some GREAT news regarding Melanie. She is out of surgery and is in stable condition. This morning, she responded to Doug's voice with tears and attempted to pull her tubes out…a real fighter. She is now heavily sedated, and as we know more, we will pass on more. THANK YOU for your prayers…keep them coming. She and her family need them now…so do not let up!"

I have also been told she recognized her mother's voice. Things are most definitely improving. Thank you to everyone for your continued prayers and outpouring of love and support. It has been incredible to see the response from all over the country and world.—Chris

3 p.m. (AZ Time) 7/29/10—John J. Jakubczyk of Arizona Right to Life e-mailed this note: "Just spoke with Melanie's mom. Melanie recognized her and was alert. She is being weaned off of the medications that were helping her heart

and lungs. She continues to need our prayers as there are some additional hurdles—BUT—all is looking so much better. THANK YOU all for your prayers. Our God is a mighty God. He reigns and His mercy endures forever. Give thanks to Our Lord for hearing our prayers and to Our Blessed Mother and all the angels and saints for their intercession. And special thumbs up to St. Anthony and St. Philomena."

5 p.m. (AZ TIME) 7/29/10—Kemi Ndolo just posted this update to Facebook with a request for specific prayers: "Pray for a very exhausted husband and father, Doug. Melanie is at one hospital, Gabriella is at another hospital, and Brady is away from both parents for now. Doug is beyond physical and emotional exhaustion, but he is staying strong for his family. A Facebook page and website will be up soon where you can support them with cards, financially, and with prayers. Help spread the word."

8 p.m. (AZ time) 7/29/10—Kemi Ndolo gave another wonderful update: "Melanie is off ventilators and talking. It is a miracle but not a surprise because miracles can and do happen. Continue to pray for the Pritchards. There will be a website and a method to help financially offset what will be some astounding medical bills. More on that tomorrow. Praise Him."[3]

The Henrys

Mark Henry's wife, Tina, and I have become close over the past few years. I have assisted her in the Pure Fashion program she runs locally. Tina's sacrifice and attitude of service is incredibly admirable. I look up to her in so many ways and consider her family as part of my own. I always tell people that Tina is my biggest fan. She only sees me with rose-colored glasses and refuses to accept that I have real faults…which I do—trust me! The fact that she and her family rushed to the hospital to sit in the waiting room to pray for me and support my family, speaks to their sincere servant hearts. The Henrys brought my family food so they would not be hungry. When I was awake, they came to see me and showered me with gifts to further uplift my spirits. Their daughter, Alyssa, knitted Ella a blanket while sitting at the hospital. She also gave me a hat that said, "One Tough Chick." This was a great gift because my hair had not been washed in days, so a hat was the perfect cover for it. All in all, seeing the Henrys was a great comfort to me.

Mark was so inspired by what he witnessed through my recovery that he wrote an article to spread the word about the miracle. Mark Henry is a Catholic writer, author, and speaker. He is also a contributing writer for Catholic Online (*www.catholic.org*), which is where the article first appeared. Like Chris's article, Mark's got picked up and posted on several other popular websites.

Pope John Paul II's Intercession

Mark's article was called "Pray It Forward: Melanie Pritchard's Miraculous Recovery." He included a picture of me in the hospital with oxygen tubes in my nose holding my dear Ella for the first time. The article revealed my recovery and gave updated information about how I survived everything that happened. The article spoke of how his family found out about my sudden death and their frantic, prayer-filled drive to the hospital. Mark shared how the family contacted everyone they could to pray for me. He said:

> I called contacts I had in Catholic media, both new and traditional. Fortunately, I got through to close friends

at Immaculate Heart Radio, St. Joseph Communications, and other Catholic media outlets who faithfully responded and immediately started broadcasting prayer requests for Melanie on the radio, Internet, and other media. I am a contributing writer for Catholic Online and a member of the Catholic Online Writers Circle. The other members joined the cascade of prayer being offered for Melanie. Of course, Melanie's friends and family had already made impassioned pleas for prayer to many convents, monasteries, and religious orders.

Very quickly news of Melanie's critical condition spread like a digital wildfire with "prayer for Melanie" requests now going "viral" online. The pray it forward juggernaut to save Melanie had begun in earnest with many specifically praying for Pope John Paul II's intercession to save the life of his loyal spiritual daughter, Melanie.[4]

When I returned home and read hundreds of e-mails and letters, what resounded with me was how many people said they had prayed for Pope John Paul II's intercession. Once I re-read these articles, it made sense why so many people had called upon this great pope to pray for me.

About two weeks after I got home, a radio station on the east coast contacted me for an interview. Honestly, I was still fragile and my memory was still suffering. I probably should not have done it. Nonetheless, I did and the host asked me point blank, "Do you think you are one of the miracles for Pope John Paul II's canonization?" Mark's article had suggested that maybe I was. The question caught me off guard, and I had to scramble to respond. I said, "That would be an incredible honor if God willed it someday. But the truth is, I know all my favorite saints and angels were there praying for me and protecting me." It was incredibly beautiful to hear many people did turn to my hero, Holy Father Pope John Paul II, to intercede on my behalf. He has always given me great strength, and I do not doubt for one second that he was standing right next to my bedside, praying for me every step of the way.

Chris's article was the first to encourage people to pray to John Paul II, and when I asked him what prompted him to request people to pray for John Paul II's intercession, he told me it is what came to him in prayer but it also came from something Mary Beth Bonacci wrote about me on her Facebook page. I have never met Mary Beth, but I called her to find out why she was inspired to pray for his intercession. She said that while she was praying for me, she had a vision of John Paul II's cloak. It was so clear that she could see the details in the fabric, and it was as if she could feel his cloak upon her face.

At the hospital, during my critical hours, my husband prayed for John Paul II's intercession while so many others were calling upon him as well. One man sent this note to Doug in an e-mail days after the incident: "At the Mt. Carmel prayer service Wednesday, I had an image in my mind as I prayed to John Paul II for Melanie's miraculous healing. John Paul II was kneeling, vested but with his head uncovered, with his back to me, as so many of us have seen him in countless pictures. His left hand reached down to Melanie in her bed; his right hand reached out to Jesus as he interceded for her. My prayer was 'Holy Father, be the bridge.'"

In addition, the first ever National Theology of the Body Congress began on July 28, and during Janet Smith's talk, the speakers and audience stopped to pray for me, calling upon John Paul II. What a powerful place to have people praying for John Paul II's intercession— at the first ever United States conference dedicated to his body of work. Moreover, the conference was being broadcast over the radio, so listeners all over the country stopped and prayed as well. Matter of fact, that is how my parish priest found out that I was in critical condition.

It is clear that John Paul II's intercession that day was a powerful force in my rapid healing and recovery! Hearing about all the prayers and all the outreach for me when I was in the hospital was a great comfort. It lifted my spirits and brought me an indescribable amount of joy as I tried to recover enough to be released from the hospital. I drew from the strength of all the prayers sent my way. Everything I had learned about the strength of prayer, especially in the sacraments, was vividly revealed to me through this outpouring.

Saints

As I read through people's e-mails and Facebook posts, in which many called upon saints to intercede on my behalf, it was clear that an army of saints and angels surrounded me during my ordeal. Hearing about this and knowing the outcome of my story, I have become a believer in the power of saintly prayer. Now, when people ask me for prayers, I don't hesitate to ask the Holy Father and other saints to intercede.

At the hospital I was given saint relics, which I brought home with me. In addition, soon after I came home, a friend brought me a first class relic of St. Gerard, patron of expectant mothers. For the first three months of my recovery, every night I prayed that these saints, whose relics were in my house, would pray for my recovery. I pressed each of the relics against my chest and prayed that the Lord would heal my heart completely.

The Miracles That Followed

In Mark's article, he spoke of miracles that came from people hearing my story. He said:

> Inspirational stories of personal faith conversions of those hearing and reading about Melanie's faithful fight for life ...started coming in. Melanie's friend Brooke told us about the man in the Midwest who had never attended church, but read the e-mail appeal for prayers for Melanie and was so inspired that he went in to the nearest church to pray. Brooke's sister Meghan told us of the security guard at the hospital who was a lifelong Catholic who had never been to adoration before; but after hearing about Melanie, he went to the adoration chapel and spent the night on his knees in prayer. Father John Parks excitedly told us about the long confession lines after the prayer vigil for Melanie at Mt. Carmel Parish in Tempe, Arizona.[5]

These were just the first of many miracles people informed me about when I returned home. The maid of honor at my wedding, Sarah, and I met 15 years ago the first day of college at Arizona State University. The day before I coded, Sarah traveled to the east coast for a family vacation. When she caught word about me, she hopped on two planes to get back to me. After I was released, she said to me, "I never truly believed in the power of prayer until this happened to you. It was unbelievable to see the community of love surrounding you all around the world. Prayer vigils, social media updates, donations, websites and more. Everyone was praying for you. It was like the world stopped to embrace you." She revealed that this experience renewed her faith in God and reminded her of how fragile life is and how she needs to live for today and always remember how blessed she is. As more friends and strangers told me their stories about finding out what happened, they expressed their awe over the great power of prayer, too.

A girl I went to grade school with and had not seen or talked to in close to 15 years found me on Facebook and wrote this:

> I have followed your postings and the blog you wrote about all that happened to you while having your baby. I have to say, this incident, though horrible for you, was an awakening for my family and a renewal in our faith. It prompted me to sign my son up for RE classes at our church, and he loves it.

A college girl came up to me at a Matt Maher concert I attended four months after returning home and said, "I prayed for you and followed your story." She said she sent out requests to her friends to pray for me and one of her friends, who grew up Catholic but was not really practicing anymore, was so inspired by the miracle of my story that she has gone back to Mass every Sunday.

I cannot even begin to tell you how many people have told me similar stories of conversions about themselves, their friends, their family, and their co-workers. I do not know what to say or how to respond because, really, I had nothing to do with it.

What is most amazing to me is that in my ministry I speak in order to lead wandering, questioning hearts back to the Lord. What I find most ironic is that the time when I have led the most people back to the Lord—inspiring thousands to pray and even come back to the Church—I did not speak a word—I was silent—completely unconscious. It is amazing how the Lord chooses to use us. All I can do is tell people how great the Lord is, how great the power of prayer is, and how God can work through suffering to bring about hope and healing.

Chapter Thirteen
Home, Sweet Home

I do not remember the first thing I saw or did when I
woke up from the incident. It is all a big haze. In fact,
the whole hospital stay is a haze. I remember holding Ella
a lot, and seeing lots of family, friends, doctors, and nurses.
I remember trying to do whatever I had to in order to go
home to be with my kids. While I was in a great deal of
pain, I persevered to make it appear that I was fine and
able to go home. It worked! After a stay of only six days, I
was released.

When I got home and I started to comprehend more
about what happened, I became afraid. I started to panic at
the thought that at any moment I could experience sudden
death again. I did not realize how comforting it was to be
in a hospital surrounded by lifesavers! I wanted to call my
doctors and tell them to admit me back into the hospital. I
was so uncertain about my health that I had no confidence
I would wake up in the morning. It was terrifying. I was
waiting for the other shoe to drop.

The Spirit of Death

While Doug and I were dating, we took a class
called "Inner and Spiritual Healing," where we learned a
tremendous amount about spiritual warfare. We learned that
when traumatic things happen in our lives, spirits can attach

themselves to us and oppress us or keep a stronghold on us. It was clear to me the spirit of death was attaching itself to me and I needed strong prayer to remove its grip. I called my prayer warrior friend Bonnie to come over and pray with Doug and me. Bonnie has incredible gifts, so I knew she would not only be able to spiritually cut the bond this spirit created with me, but she would also be able to use her gifts to help me understand where the Lord was calling me after this traumatic incident.

An Exposed Heart

Bonnie said some incredibly revealing and wise things during this prayer session, but the most notable was this: She said that throughout my speaking ministry, I always relied on my head knowledge to give talks, but this traumatic experience was going to change my ministry and my talks. She explained they were no longer going to come from my head; they would now come from my heart. At the time, I thought about my physical heart—it was weak and not functioning as it should. I thought about how just a few weeks prior, the doctors considered putting me on a heart transplant list and there was still talk about needing a defibrillator placed in my chest to shock my heart if it should ever fail. I had a vision of God breaking my physical heart to release my emotional one.

The truth? My heart has been walled and calloused for years. There is only so much pain a heart can take before it goes into defense mode. My speaking career and ministry changed my heart. When I hear story after story of woman after woman aborting her child or aborting four children because no one ever told them it was a life, or how they now regret this terrible mistake and are crying on my shoulder, it takes a toll. When I hear teenager after teenager tell me the incredible pain in their lives, pain that they should never have to feel so young, it takes a toll on my heart. It was either weep inconsolably after hearing about each person's deep-rooted pain, or harden my heart. I hardened my heart. But the sad thing is that when I hardened my heart for one area of my life, it affected all areas. It is the same heart I showed to my family and friends because I could not just switch the wall off and on whenever I saw fit. Ultimately, that hardness affected all of my relationships. To some extent, I was emotionless. Few have ever seen me cry because I do not cry. When people told me horrible things, I had empathy and sympathy for them, but I cut off the emotional side of me and tapped into my logical side in order to counsel them. It is how I coped.

So what was God doing here? Since I awoke from death, my emotional heart felt open and exposed—naked. How would I speak without crying? How would I listen to someone else's pain without truly feeling it? Is God asking me to continue my ministry with an exposed heart? All I can do is trust that for whatever reason God broke my heart physically and emotionally that he replaced it with a bigger and stronger one—one that will help me be an honest representation of myself.

Bonnie's prayers that day set me free from my fears. She prayed against the evil attaching itself to me and instantly I felt free and excited to be alive. I no longer felt like every minute could be my last. Rather, I felt every minute was a gift I needed to live fully.

Falling Apart

Those first few weeks were incredibly difficult as I was on quite a few medications. My memory was still not fully intact, and I was weak and in a lot of pain. All my defenses were down. Things that normally bother me, like my son eating food off the dirty ground or ten different germy people holding my newborn in a day, did not faze me. I had bigger problems. I was in pain, I had 50 staples holding my stomach together, I was unable to hold Ella for long periods of time, and I was given strict instructions from the doctors not to lift Brady. I felt so disconnected from my own children, especially Brady.

Brady had been without me for almost a week, so he acted very distant toward me. He actually wanted nothing to do with me. I wanted to love him the way he needed to be loved; but at the same time, I was physically unable to do anything. I thought it was almost better that he was distant, that he preferred others over me because then, at least, his feelings would not be hurt if he could not get close to me.

He was also acting up. I assume being away from his dad and me, along with having a new sister, does that to a two-and-a-half year old. There were many times when he would throw a fit and scream and cry. I did not have the physical and emotional strength to handle it, so I would just fall down and cry myself. He would cry, I would cry, and sometimes Ella would cry. I just gave up. I was weak, I was scared, and these were thoughts and emotions foreign to me. I knew I was falling apart. The only thing that helped my sanity was my mother being there every day, all day, and my amazing friends who gave her breaks in the day. They held Ella and played with Brady while I lay on the couch unable to participate. I was grateful to them for helping me.

Trying to Control the Chaos

People were overwhelmingly generous with their time. When they were there with me, it was understood they were in charge and they had to take care of both kids and had the right to discipline Brady. I wanted everyone to do whatever they needed to do to survive this chaotic situation with me. Some friends felt weird about disciplining my child, but Brady acted out so much, it had to be done. Of course my friends were all very loving about it, but, nonetheless, I am sure it was hard for them. I gave my mom full permission to take over every aspect of my life to make it through each day, even if that meant Brady watching four hours of cartoons to keep him occupied, something I would normally not permit.

My mom was amazing. She managed to take care of the children, take care of me, and even do all the chores around the house. Her strength and perseverance inspired me every day, although she and I cried often. We started a running count of how long we could go without crying. I think there was one day in three months when we actually got through a day without tears. Sometimes we cried about all the pain I was in, sometimes we cried after someone shared a story of how they prayed for me, or sometimes we cried just because we were so joyful about how fast I was recovering. Whatever it was, our emotions were running high.

Chapter Fourteen
SHARING MY THOUGHTS

*M*any people wrote to tell me of their prayers, and asked for updates, so I began to blog. Blogging was great because it forced me to sit down and process the way I felt. I was probably more honest in those blogs than I might have been in person. Blogging is interesting. It sort of tricked me into thinking I was journaling. I revealed my innermost, private thoughts and feelings and made them accessible for the public to see. I had blogged about teaching topics before, but never had I blogged about my emotional state until then. I guess what changed my heart about blogging about my situation was that I no longer felt like the people reading my postings were strangers. I felt that, because they prayed for me, we were connected—I considered them friends—friends whose names I did not know and whose faces I had not seen, but friends nevertheless. I know it sounds weird, but those friends' prayers saved my life and gave me strength in my darkest moments.

On August 8, 2010, I wrote a blog entitled *Eleven Days Ago the Lord Spared My Life*. Looking back, I do not know how I even wrote in that condition, but I knew I had to get something out to all those who had been praying for me. In the blog, I recapped what took place at the hospital and shared my thoughts about the evil one. I stated, "I firmly believe the evil one had a plan that day to take my life; but God's infinite mercy, the hands of incredible doctors and surgeons, my priest friends who brought me Communion, and the faithful community with incredibly selfless love, support, and prayers squashed whatever plans he had."

I concluded the blog by sharing about a Mass held in my home and by thanking those who stood by me.

> Last night, my good friend Father John Muir celebrated Mass in my house for my family since I am homebound for a while during recovery. He said the most profound words in his homily. The second reading was the story of Abraham and Isaac. God asked Abraham to sacrifice his son's life and Abraham was ready to do it. In the end, God stopped Abraham from killing his son, but Abraham had shown an incredible trust in God's plan.

> Eleven days ago, Father Muir, with the assistance of my other great friend Father Parks, administered the sacrament of Anointing of the Sick on me in the hospital. Last night, in his homily, he spoke of how my mother, my father, my husband, my brother, and my sisters were much like Abraham when they were asked to say their goodbyes to me that night and to trust that God had a bigger plan. God gave me back to them and to all of you as a symbol of God's trustworthiness, his resurrection, his power, and his grace.

> Each one of you who has stayed by my side in prayer, who kept up with my recovery, and who sent me letters, Facebook entries, Tweets, and e-mails, I thank you. I will pray for you, my faithful friends and community! You truly changed my life! Thank you!

Two weeks later, on August 22, 2010, I updated everyone with a second blog entitled *The Greatest Miracle*. I was beginning to understand and process more of what happened, especially when it came to the amount of people who prayed for me. It inspired me to write more. The following is some of what I shared.

When I was in a high school church youth group, the question was posed, "If you were on your deathbed, who would you need to call or what would you need to take care of?" Hands raised as people responded with an assortment of things; however, one wise person answered, "I would not need to call anyone or do anything because I live every day as if it is the last." That response always stuck in my brain.

Now that I have experienced death, I have to ask myself the same question posed in high school. I have asked myself many other questions, too. Did I love my husband enough? Did he know it? Did my children know their worth and how much they meant to me? Did my family feel my love and respect for them? Did my friends know how much I cared about them? Was I a good friend? Was I a good citizen? Was I true to myself and my word? Did I make a difference in this world? Was I faithful to God and to living my life in a way pleasing to him? These questions and more are ones I have come face-to-face with during my days of recovery. The answers to all of these questions are that I tried my best to be a good wife, a good mother, a good family member, a good friend, a good citizen, one who is true to her word, and faithful to God.

Had I died, I could have died in peace knowing nothing went unsaid and knowing I lived an exciting life for the Lord with the ability to make a difference in this world. Why God chose to keep me alive is one thing only the future will reveal as I feel a renewed purpose. Maybe my death was an awakening for me to simplify my life or an awakening that God has more plans to use me, or maybe it was an awakening for me not just to "be." Maybe I was a pawn in a bigger plan God had to bring others to their knees in prayer, to rely solely on him, to realize their limitations and inability to control life's events. Maybe it was a reality check. God is in control, he is in charge, and he wants his children to come home to him by falling to their knees, pounding their fists in the air, and praying to him with unceasing devotion. Maybe this was not about me. Maybe this was about all of us.

...What I have witnessed back in this life is truly the most beautiful! And the greatest miracle was not that God brought me back to life, but that he brought so many back to him through this situation. A community of people around the world came together for a moment in time to pray, to hold their families a little closer, to believe in the impossible, and to believe miracles can happen. If this is all that ever comes from what I endured, it will be enough to know the human condition is good, wonderful, and beautiful. We have the ability to love a stranger in ways maybe we never knew were possible. We are truly God's children, connected by our inheritance given to us by the greatest lover and maker of all time...our Father in heaven.

I had to write this blog because I was overwhelmed by people's generosity and wanted to let them know their prayers and support mattered to me. I will never get tired of hearing their stories.

I had every intention of writing blogs every few weeks, but the day after this last blog, I developed the infection clostridium difficile (C. diff) which made survival nearly impossible. I had no memory of the fatal delivery and hospital recovery and I did not remember the severity of pain I endured; but this new infection was the worst thing I ever "remember" happening to me. I do not know how to describe it other than to say it was terrible and awful and truly tested my mental, emotional, and physical strength. It was so bad that in addition to the infection, I contracted thrush, a yeast infection on my tongue, probably a side effect of the antibiotics. Thrush made me feel like I had hair stuck in the back of my throat all the time. It was incredibly bothersome and lasted for at least two months because I did not have the energy or time to deal with it. I was so sick with the infection and still recovering from surgery that having thrush felt like a minor thing to worry about. I had to pick my health battles, and that was not one of them. Finally, after three months had passed and the infection was gone, I sat down to reflect and write. Many people had requested an update and I thought they truly deserved my honest, raw emotion. Here is what I wrote.

October 18, 2010, The Last Three Months

This week marks three months since my amniotic fluid embolism. On Friday, I will go back to the hospital for an ECHO of my heart. This will be the moment I find out if I can take off the defibrillator. If my heart has not recovered, they will place a defibrillator in my chest. I am feeling good these days and am confident my heart has recovered. We will soon see!

It has been a while since I have blogged, and part of that has to do with being busy raising my two children; but the other part is I did not even know where to begin to write about all that has happened and all that I have gone through. This will hopefully shed some light on the past three months.

About a week after I returned home from the hospital, a nurse called from the hospital where I delivered Ella to check up on me. She explained that even though I could not remember the nurses that attended to me, they remembered me and it would mean the world to them if I ever had the chance to stop by the hospital. Hearing that, I grabbed my husband, my father-in-law (who was staying with us at the time), and the kids and jumped in the car to surprise the nurses. When we arrived, a few nurses ran to gather all the other nurses. Some of them were weeping and hugging me and asking me all kinds of questions I did not know the answers to because I had no memory of the incident. From the looks on their faces, what happened to me had impacted their lives. The hardest thing for me was not remembering something I was involved in, something that made these total strangers break down and cry.

A representative from the hospital asked me if I would be willing to come back to speak to their hospital leadership team about my experiences. I agreed and returned about a week later to what I thought would be a small meeting with hospital board members. A staff member escorted me to the boardroom; and as we approached, a woman walked along side us heading toward the meeting as well. When she heard the other woman call me Melanie, she stopped, fell against the wall, gasped for air and looked intently at my face. She began to cry as she recognized that it was me. It did not take long for me to realize showing up would be a healing experience for those who cared for me. They needed to see me alive. The last time they saw me, I was leaving in an ambulance for another hospital and the certainty of my survival was slim. They never received the closure they deserved after all they had been through.

When I walked in, I found that there were over 100 doctors, nurses, and staff crammed into a small boardroom. Some, I heard later, were turned away because there was no more room. Again I heard people weeping and tissues being taken out. My husband, mother, sister Kym, baby Ella, and I were introduced. A staff member recapped my story for the audience and then allowed my family and me to tell our perspective. After we shared, the hospital representative told me to look behind me, where there were about thirty or forty people standing. She explained that all of those people helped in my care. I was amazed at the army it took to save my life. Each person then told me how they helped. As they spoke, I looked them in the eyes, I shook their hands, and I said, "Thank you."

It was a moment I will never forget. The anesthesiologist, doctors, and staff that performed CPR on me; the nurse who was at my side; the doctor who delivered Ella; the intensive care doctor; and the doctor who performed my surgeries all grabbed and hugged me tight with tears in their eyes. The intensive care physician asked me if I remembered him and for some reason, he looked familiar. Then he explained that he came and sat with me when I was recovering at the new hospital. I did remember him coming to visit and I remembered thinking, who is this guy hanging out in my room? It was this new encounter with him that made me realize that he cared so much for me, he came to visit me on his time. I never knew doctors to be like this. I had never felt so much love from strangers.

As we were leaving, another staff member told me when I was there, a housekeeping staff member came in to clean the room I had been in during the trauma; as she entered, she saw an incredible amount of empty bags of blood on the floor. She immediately got the rest of her crew to come in and pray for the woman who had lost all this blood. They thought there was no way I could have survived, but they came in and prayed for me...a total stranger. But to them, I was no stranger. They were not just doing their jobs that day; they were invested in me as a person instead of a mere patient. It is this kind of story that has made such an imprint on my life.

The day I came back from revisiting the hospital staff, I began experiencing symptoms from an infection I had contracted while still in the hospital and on antibiotics. My road to recovery was still a struggle. The infection was so bad; I lost a great deal of weight daily. I could not eat or drink and was becoming dehydrated, which is not good for anyone...let alone someone with heart problems. I was weak and tired; I could not hold my daughter or play with my son. At first I thought I was not feeling well because of the medications I was on or because of the surgeries. After about a week of my health not improving, I finally went to Urgent Care because I knew I would not be able to reach my brother since he had a full day of surgery.

The doctor did not give me any answers and I went home. I told Doug if I die again, know that I have lived a good life and go on without me. That should reveal to you the state I was in. I did not think I would make it through this time. I was distraught and weeping uncontrollably for hours, wondering how I could possibly get through this illness. I did not have the strength. The next day, a friend came to see me, took one look at me, and said, "We're getting you to a doctor." She made a phone call to a friend of hers who is a doctor since I did not have a primary care doctor. He said he could get me in right away. I knew I had to go, but I did not know if I could muster up the strength for the car ride. I pushed through the pain and got into her car.

She drove me to her friend's office, where I was seen by a Catholic doctor who immediately put me on an IV of fluids to help with my dehydration. He diagnosed me with C. diff, the same infection my brother suspected I had. It was also the infection my grandfather had died of just a few days earlier, an infection he contracted from the hospital as well. This was even more concerning because I had just witnessed my grandfather suffer through this terrible illness, ultimately leading to his death soon after I had returned home from the hospital. I was scared I, too, would die — that the other shoe would drop, that what happened at the hospital was just the beginning. I thought, maybe I am not intended to live. Keep in mind, I was on a lot of pain medication and had a hormonal imbalance from just having a baby. My thoughts were not clear and I was depressed. This doctor and my brother finally put me on the right track to healing. It took several weeks to cure, and I suffered tremendously during that time, but it drew me ever so close to the Lord. Every time I suffered, I offered it up for others, and I prayed constantly. All I could do was pray. All I could do was ask others to pray. All I could do was trust in the Lord. Once again, I was able to make it through and I did recover.

My mother has come to take care of me every day, all day, for the past three months. She has literally given up her life to take care of me and the children to make sure I do not overexert my heart. My emotional heart bursts every day I see her. It is as if an angel walks through my door every morning. Motherhood is a sacrifice and I know that, but when you are on the other end of that sacrifice, it is hard to comprehend this kind of selfless love. There has not been a day gone by that she does not well up with tears recalling what happened to me. I hate that her heart hurts from the pain of watching me go through all I did. I know she relates to the pain of Mary, watching her child die and unable to control it. I can only imagine how I would feel in her shoes. I cherish every moment with her.

My mom catches me gazing at her sometimes and cannot figure out why I am always looking at her. I guess it is because I love her so much and am so grateful for her; I am etching her in my memory, sitting there with me and loving me beyond measure. I never want these memories to go away. I want them to stay with me forever. She need not say a word and I know I am loved. She is training me, through her example, in how to love my children so completely I would forsake myself. I am a better mother because she has mothered me so well. My mom has endured too much these past three months. She witnessed my trauma, and a few days after I returned home, her father died and her mother was diagnosed with cancer. In addition, my mother has not been able to spend the kind of time with my brother's new baby that she does with Ella. I know this breaks her heart. I am starting the canonization process for her!

My husband is another I am signing up for canonization. Before we were married, people asked what made me fall in love with Doug, and one of my responses was that if ever I was on my deathbed, he would be the guy standing next to me holding my hand and looking at me with a kind of love that never fades. Who knew that day would come only three years into our marriage? Doug has endured too much, as well. His strength is one only a true man of God could have. At the beginning of my recovery, I was unable to care for the children, so not only did he have to go to work, he had to come home and take on the responsibilities of caring for the kids, taking care of me, and running the household. At our wedding, the priest said, "Today should be the day you love each other the least. Every year, your love should grow more than the year before." Wow! He said it best. I love my husband a thousand times more today than the day we were married. He is my superhero!

Not only have my mother and husband sacrificed for me, but all my friends and family have, too. They took turns coming in a few hours a day to give my mom breaks. They brought much joy to my life. Since I was homebound for most of my recovery, knowing they were coming over livened me up, and Brady, too! I am especially grateful to my neighbor Tifni who, when I was at my sickest, would take Brady to her house to play with her children to give him a sense of normalcy and to give my mother and me a break. She is another saint in the making! My father helped us by taking over for my mom at times, helping my husband with things around the house, and helping my brother and his wife with their new baby while my mom was with us. He has such a giving heart! I am blessed to have the most wonderful family and friends who have stepped in during my time of need to be there for me in whatever ways I needed. I have a grateful heart!

Today, someone I have not seen in years came up to me and did the same thing so many others have been doing. He took in a deep breath, looked into my eyes with the most loving gaze, and said, "It is so good to see you," and then gave me the biggest bear hug. This is an everyday occurrence in my life since the trauma and this love is something I wish every person could experience. I told Doug today that when all of this is behind us, and as people forget, I will miss the look in their eyes when they see me.

I used to have such a hard heart and tough exterior, but this has changed me. It has softened me. The Lord has pierced my heart in ways that I cannot hide from anymore. The cares I used to have disappeared, and all I want to do is live even more for the Lord and to be a witness for his Truth. I have become a total mush-ball! I feel like in dying and coming back to life, the walled-off, calloused parts of me have died. God has peeled back the layers of me as if peeling an onion and my core is exposed. The Lord has given me an invitation to start anew and to regain sight of what is most important. For me, it took dying to awaken me to God's plan for my life instead of my plan.

I have gone from being a strong and independent woman, to a woman who is weak and vulnerable. I have let down my guard and allowed others to serve me and take care of me. I have died to be set free from restrictions I placed on myself. God has done to me what he has done to the Eucharist. He has taken me, broken me, and blessed me, so I may share what I know with the world.

When I was at my worst, I kept my spirits up by dreaming about being on a beach playing with my children. I would also repeat over and over to myself, "In three months, I bet things will improve. If I can just get to that point, life will be better." When three months passed, I *was* remarkably better. The infection was finally gone. My lungs improved. I could breathe easier. I had more energy. My heart was healing. I went back to "work" and gave a chastity talk to 200 junior high students at a Lutheran school. About a week after giving that talk, Doug and I took the kids to the outdoor mall. After we got home, I posted this on Facebook: "Today is a day I dreamed of. Walked around Tempe Marketplace with the fam. So simple, but not something I have been able to do until today. I'm tired, but boy, am I glad to be alive!" Going through this experience has given me a greater sense of hope in all things I do. It truly is the simplest things that I appreciate now.

Hope Comes from Sharing

Many people wrote Doug and I sharing their emotions about how our honesty in these blogs and in radio and TV interviews touched their lives. Many identified with our suffering, and some found hope and healing from hearing our accounts. One woman shared this incredible story with me.

> A year and a half ago I was a victim of a violent crime. I was robbed and shot in the chest with a 9mm. The bullet traveled across my chest, missed my heart by one cm, tore my esophagus and my lungs collapsed from the fragments of the bullet hitting them. The doctors all said it's a miracle I'm alive and that I should have dropped dead the moment the bullet entered my body. I truly believe that the miracle of my life is the result of the prayers of the universal church! To this day I cannot believe how fast the news of this incident traveled! Anyway, because of this tragedy and going through the process of intense physical recovery and reliving the trauma during the trial, I have come to have compassion and love again!
>
> I too have been suffering from an infection since my incident. I have had it for a year and a half and haven't

been able to figure out exactly what it is and how to treat it. While I offer up my suffering for different people every time it flares up and I'm in pain, it has been a huge struggle lately to not become impatient and frustrated that I'm not healed yet, and scared at what is ravaging my body. But while you were sharing, I was reminded that there is a purpose to suffering and that I need to embrace it even when it seems to have no end in sight.

What I find amazing is the comfort that comes from sharing our suffering. This woman's story gave me hope, and made me believe in the power of prayer—even more! My story may have brought her comfort, but her story did the same for me. We are strangers, but somehow our suffering has united us! She also shared with me the that her heart had become hardened doing ministry as well, and like me, God broke her heart, too, physically, emotionally, and spiritually. But through all her suffering, God has restored her heart "to have compassion and love again." To hear how God is using my story to help others find hope makes everything I went through worth it! This too was sent to me from another man suffering.

> I have been praying for God to give me hope and your story did it. My wife divorced me after 24 years of marriage and left me and our 4 children for another man. I was recently laid off and out of work for 9 months, exhausted my savings, had health problems, my parents are in ill health, three of my children are grown and left home and I'm feeling alone and without hope. I don't understand why these things have happened and had all but given up hope when I heard your story. Thank you for giving me hope.

I am speechless when I read these kinds of stories that frequent my e-mail inbox. All I can say is, "Thank you God for using me and my story to bring others hope in healing as they suffer." All I can do is pray for them as so many have done for me!

Chapter Fifteen
Making Mistakes

When I was pregnant with Ella, I spent a lot of time with Brady working on his letters and numbers and doing crafts. After my return from the hospital, I had to surrender my desire to make Brady the smartest child alive. I just had to survive each day; it was self-preservation time. With everything that happened, I settled on knowing that he was fed and felt loved. What is ironic is that during my recovery, we let Brady watch Leapfrog episodes about the alphabet. In a month, he could recite every letter and sound. One day, he was driving with my husband and he said, "Dad, what's cccvvvssss?" as if sounding out the letters to make a word. Doug looked up and there was the cvs store. Thank you, Leapfrog! We were amazed that in the midst of all of this, our child was still learning. God was taking care of my littlest fears.

When I came home, Brady was out of sorts, but he did eventually calm down and begin to behave himself. He went from wanting to throw Ella in the trash (he would say that) to falling in love with her. Doug encouraged him to embrace the role of protective, older brother. Because I was so sick and unable to really play with Brady, Doug told him that his job was to take care of me and Ella every day while daddy was at work, so he would not feel bad when I could not attend to him. Brady began saying to people, "I'm the big brother and it is my job to take care of Momma and Ella every day." He took that job seriously, too seriously.

Six months after the incident, I noticed that my son, who was now three years old, had been forced to take on an adult role and that I needed to correct it. Brady always had to turn to someone else for his every need because I could not take care of him. Throughout all of recovery and even after, he turned to his dad for comfort and help. Even when I could finally care for him, he would get angry and push me away. It hurt my motherly heart so much, but I knew that somehow the incident, and all that surrounded it, did this to our relationship.

In the months following the incident, Brady lacked affection for me and wanted to do everything himself. I began to think that maybe his independence, one not normal for even a three-year-old, was because in his little mind he had taken to heart that he really had to take care of Mommy and Ella. We gave Brady a role he should never have had at his age, and it burdened his little heart.

Upon realizing this may be the cause, I immediately went to him and said, "Son, mommy is all better." I showed him the healed scar on my stomach, and continued, "It is now my job to take care of Brady and Ella. I am not sick anymore." He looked at me confused, trying to correct me, saying, "I take care of Mommy and Ella." I lovingly replied to him, "I am giving you a new job. Your job everyday is to be a good boy, have fun, and be like Jesus!" For the next few days, I repeated that to him over and over trying to get it to sink in. Finally, it did.

Brady was playing outside and fell on the concrete and skinned his foot. He cried and called for his father, and Doug took him in and put a Band-Aid on it. I came to him, and at first he pushed me away, and I said, "Brady, remember it is my job to take care of you, too." Doug let me take over, and I finished cleaning him up. I took him to the couch where he laid his head on my shoulder. I gently rocked him, repeating over and over, "Momma will take care of you and Ella. That is my job because I am not sick anymore." Then Brady said in a caring, quiet voice, "Momma, I will take care of you when your belly hurts." I thanked him for taking good care of me while I was sick, and reminded him again, "Momma is no longer sick. I am all better, so now I take care of you." For the first time since before the incident, Brady laid there on me for a half hour. I had to hold back tears as finally my son understood that I was capable of being there for him. He was allowing me to love him and take care of him. It was a moment I will never forget because as time had passed and the incident seemed so far away, it reminded me again of the great sacrifices that had to be made even by my son for me to recover.

I share this with you because it is one of many things I have had to correct. I never thought there would be a time when I would not be the parent I desired to be, but life happened, nothing I could ever see coming, and things got messy. Doug and I corrected the mistake of making our son feel responsible for me and Ella because it is never too late to set things straight and bring order to disordered behavior especially when it involves innocent children who get caught up in things. The mom in me wants to beat myself up for all the little mistakes I have made as a parent after returning from the hospital, but I know the devil is preying upon my fears. All I can do now is move forward in good health and be more conscious of how each decision I make affects my children.

Chapter Sixteen
WHAT THE DOCTORS SAY

*I*continued to see two cardiologists throughout my recovery. On my first visit, they were concerned with my chance for "sudden death," as one of the doctors referred to it. Because they were worried I might suffer congestive heart failure, they put me on a low salt-low liquid diet. I was only allowed to drink 64 ounces of liquid and eat 2000 milligrams of salt a day. The diet was difficult at first, but I quickly adjusted to it. I had the attitude that I could maintain any diet if it meant surviving one more day with my family, and at least they were not limiting my sugar!

The cardiologist also wanted me to wear a portable defibrillator around my chest which would shock me if my heart suddenly stopped again. If the vest did not detect a heartbeat, an alarm would sound. If I heard the alarm, I would need to press a button to delay the paddles from the shock. Even though the vest and battery pack I had to wear 24 hours a day, with the exception of showering, was incredibly uncomfortable, I was relieved to have it. It became my security blanket. The first few weeks I did not even want to shower for fear my heart would stop while I was in there without the vest.

The Alarm Sounded

One morning around 6:30 a.m., the alarm from the defibrillator sounded while I was holding Ella. Doug came running into the room and with great fear in my voice, I said, "What do I do?" He said frantically, "Push the button." I pushed the button to delay the shock, handed Ella to him, and laid down on the bed. I said, "If I'm going to pass out, I would like to be lying down." I laid there a while and took deep breaths to calm myself. I was thinking maybe I could prevent another cardiac arrest by relaxing. The alarm did not sound again, so I contacted the company to ask them what happened. They had a continuous read on my heart and after checking, they said it was a false alarm and that it was just "noise." We were overjoyed that it was not my heart. The vest went off a few more times and each time it proved to be a false alarm. The majority of the problem was that I kept losing so much weight that the vest became too loose and did not register my heartbeat properly.

The vest was hot, and I got a heat rash underneath it. The doctor said I could take it off to recover from the rash, but because I worried my heart could fail, I chose to wear it regardless of the major discomfort I felt. My top priority was staying alive! I had to wear the vest and battery pack for three-and-a-half months. And by the end of that time, I was praying my heart made a full recovery, so I could stop wearing it.

The Good News

"Oh what a beautiful morning, oh what a beautiful day" were the lyrics I was excitedly singing the day I had my echocardiogram to determine the function of my heart. Fifty-five percent is the normal ejection fraction rate. When

I left the hospital, mine was at 25 percent and the reason I had to wear the portable defibrillator. After three months of resting and recovering, my heart's ejection fraction rate returned to 65 percent, completely normal. I cannot express to you the incredible joy of hearing I had made a full recovery! The moment I heard the news, I said a prayer of thanksgiving. God made "all things new" with my heart like I knew he would! As soon as I came home, I updated the many people who had continued praying for me. Since I felt like we had all been in this together, I could not wait to give them the good news.

Amniotic Fluid Embolism

At my follow-up appointments, the cardiologists spoke about my condition and used other terms for the incident like peripartum cardiomyopathy rather than amniotic fluid embolism, the term used at the first hospital. When I questioned them about it, they said they did not believe I had an amniotic fluid embolism because I survived. Women who have AFE's die. When I researched AFE, it seemed like I had every symptom, so I could not understand why they would totally discard that as the cause. Finally it occurred to me that these doctors did not believe in miracles, so they had to come up with another diagnosis.

My ECHO showed my heart had returned to normal; however, the cardiologists wanted to do more testing to be thorough in their assessment. All the testing again showed I had made a full recovery. When one of the doctors told me the results, I said, "It's a miracle." He replied in somewhat of a perplexed tone, "It is amazing." I began to question the cardiologists again, asking if they were still ruling out an AFE. One said the tests suggested that his hypothesis about peripartum cardiomyopathy was probably not accurate given the recovery of my heart in a short amount of time, so I asked, "Then could it have been an AFE?" He said, "I won't rule it out, but whatever the cause, I feel your heart stopped because your blood pressure dropped too low." The reason I was adamant about finding the correct diagnosis is because it would determine the risk of future pregnancy. For a woman who has already suffered an AFE, to suffer another would be like getting hit by lightning twice. As I speak with other AFE survivors (and very few exist), it is as if we are telling the same story—from feeling sick, to having a seizure-like convulsion, going into cardiac arrest, DIC, and even not being able to remember anything, then waking up in total confusion just wanting to get our babies and go home.

Future Pregnancy

The doctors reiterated what they had said to me at every single appointment— under no circumstance should I ever get pregnant. They warned it could kill me or leave my heart permanently damaged. If my heart has made a full and total recovery and my risk for sudden death is the same as any woman in my age group, how can there be any greater risk for me than any other woman? I have asked the doctors that question over and over, and the response they give is they do not know how my heart will respond since pregnancy places high demands on the heart. I usually leave with more questions than I come in with. In addition, I spoke with a very qualified high-risk pregnancy doctor and asked her opinion as to whether it would be prudent for me to get pregnant again given I suffered an AFE. I explained to her what my heart went through and its rapid recovery. Her opinion was in line with my cardiologists. She too said I should never try to get pregnant for what it could do to my heart.

There are a few other AFE survivors I have contacted who have gone on to have more children without complication. But I cannot hold their cases as evidence because each AFE case is different, and we all suffered different degrees of symptoms. In addition, since I was massively transfused after the cut artery, my heart had to work harder. The other AFE survivors did not deal with that particular issue, so it is nearly impossible to find clear-cut evidence to suggest there is little or no risk in getting pregnant again.

For my husband and me to hear this news stirs up a battle in our minds and hearts. We try to come to a conclusion based on faith and reason. We have spent much time weighing these experts' opinions versus our own desires and what God wants. We always envisioned having four or five children or as many as God would give us. When the cardiologists told me not to have any more children, they said things like, "Well, you already have two children and you have your boy and girl. That's plenty." Their response was insensitive especially given how new the thought of not having more children was for me. The problem is we are not the typical modern family. We are practicing Catholics who view life as the most beautiful gift we could offer this world. Being open to life is a freedom we take seriously and not one we would forgo just because we had already been blessed with our boy and girl. Although their logic was not said in consideration of my feelings (especially in my postpartum condition), I did see their purpose. They want me to live a long life and not take chances, so they were trying to reason with me.

When we were told we should never have children again, the doctors then asked, as if it were the obvious next step, "Will you be getting your tubes tied or will your husband be getting a vasectomy?" I responded, "We will do neither as we are Catholic and both options are against our faith." Both the cardiologists looked at my husband and I like we were crazy, fanatical lunatics. I said, "We will be practicing Natural Family Planning (NFP) as our method of delaying pregnancy." It was clear by the two doctors' facial expressions they had no idea what that was. Doug went on to say, "We practice the sympto-thermal method," thinking they might understand that term. Finally one of the doctors said, "Do you mean the rhythm method?" I immediately fired back, "NFP is absolutely not the rhythm method." The main cardiologist then questioned the effectiveness of NFP, to which I responded, "It is 99 percent effective, which is better than most contraception." He asked in disbelief and with a tone of arrogance, "Where is your evidence?" He proceeded to look it up on the computer right then and there to prove me wrong. I told him I would bring the evidence and the studies to him. He said he would like to see such evidence. I was completely shocked that these doctors did not know about Natural Family Planning.

Later, I collected all the evidence I needed to prove NFP's effectiveness and took it to him. Whether he read it or not was up to him. My sincere desire was that he will educate himself on healthy alternatives to contraception or sterilization. Right before I left his office I said, "I really hope you read this information because if you ever treat another woman in child-bearing age, you might inform her about NFP. NFP does not cause cancer as some contraceptives do."

Will We Have More Children?

The doctors also insisted on keeping me on the heart medication I have taken since I was in the hospital. They indicated that they want to keep me on it for at least a year, maybe two. Unfortunately, the medication can cause birth defects if I were to get pregnant, so with that news and the fear the doctors have about my heart in future pregnancy, we must avoid pregnancy.

There are so many great things that have come from this incident, and I can recognize all the ways God has worked in this, but knowing if I were to get pregnant there is a chance I could die or suffer more heart problems is by far the worst aftereffect. The ability to give life to another human being is the greatest gift; to be told we can no longer participate in creation, something I hold as my sacred freedom, is heartbreaking.

Doug and I committed on our wedding day to be open to children, so we will continue to be open—however, now we will just be open to adopting children. We have prayed that if the Lord wills it, he will drop a child into our laps, so to speak. We will not necessarily actively seek it out right at the moment, but we are ready and willing if the Lord presents the opportunity.

About eight months after the incident, I received a message from a woman whose niece was going to have an abortion. She asked if I could intercede. I saw that the e-mail was left late Wednesday night while I was sleeping and I only got it on Thursday morning. I attempted to reach the woman at 8 a.m. only to get her machine. I left a message saying I would like to help her niece make the right decision and to call me immediately. I did not hear back. I prayed and thought about this young girl often throughout the day hoping at any moment I would receive a phone call. As the previous Education Director for Life Educational Corporation, I had many of these conversations with women before, but this time I felt more anxious and impatient. At 1:00 p.m., I decided to call the woman again. She answered, and I heard a sad tone as she said those words I did not want to hear, "My niece already had the abortion this morning. The baby is dead."

I felt like I got punched in the gut. I told the woman that I would still like to speak with her niece to help her not make this same choice again and to offer her options for healing like Rachel's Vineyard. After we hung up, sadness loomed over me. It seemed like I was having a selfish, yet selfless sadness as I thought, "I would have adopted that baby."

If only I could have turned back the clock just a few hours to meet with this pregnant woman, sit her down, hear her story, and tell her mine. I would have encouraged her to be heroic—to offer this human being growing inside of her a life. And if she wasn't willing or able to care for her child herself, I wanted her to be able to look into my eyes, to see my authentic willingness not only to love her, but her child as well. If only she could have heard my story, she would have sensed that my heart could have loved her child immeasurably. I know I could have convinced her to keep her child.

This may sound weird, but I feel like I lost a child that day. I know the child was not mine, but he or she could have been. For several days I was in mourning for that soul whose life was taken shortly after it began. I imagine my efforts in saving babies will take on a whole new meaning now that I have survived my AFE and have been advised not to have any children of my own. I imagine that every child I cannot save I will view as losing one of my own—one that my husband and I would have taken into our home and introduced to his or her new brother and sister, Brady and Ella. We could have been that child's family. Oh how my heart aches for that lost child and for the millions more lost to this selfish act. My heart aches for others who can only be open to life by means of adoption—for those waiting for the day a woman makes the heroic decision not to abort her baby and to give that child a life by placing him or her in the hands of people who have the capacity to love beyond measure.

The very same woman who shared that heart wrenching news with me also told me something that warmed my heart. She told me that she knew to contact me to see if I would intercede because she had been at the hospital while I was in critical condition. I was taken aback by this, as I did not know her. She said that while she was in the waiting room, she overheard a young man ask my sister how I was doing. My sister inquired how he knew me and he shared that he did not know me personally, but he heard about what happened on Facebook. He then told her that I had come to his school to give a talk about abortion when his girlfriend was pregnant. This young man said he and his girlfriend had planned to abort their baby until they heard my talk. He came to the hospital to tell me that I was the reason their baby lived and their child is now three years old.

As I have spent much of my life educating on the reality of abortion and trying to save lives, I realize that there are babies that I have probably helped save, but never have I seen the face of one of those children or heard from a couple like this one, who came to be at the hospital with me.

This phone conversation was surreal. While my heart was breaking over the child that just lost his or her life, in the same conversation, I found out that I saved a life I never knew about.

Whenever I am confused or distraught, I invite the Lord in to reveal himself in the circumstance at hand, so I did, wondering why all this, in the same conversation. Was the Lord trying to encourage my discouraged heart? Was he allowing me to see that my work does save lives, and that I must continue? What I do know is that the Lord has ignited an even bigger passion for me to save lives by making it personal—by allowing me to see a glimpse of the pain God feels when one of his children loses their life to abortion.

Chapter Seventeen

FORGIVENESS

Living everyday as though it is my last is something I think about often. I want to live with no regrets. I felt that had I died, I would have been comfortable knowing I really did not have people in my life with whom there were words unsaid. I am a really honest person, so people in my life know where they stand with me.

I had a friend who lied to Doug and me about some important matters. We confronted him about it and thought we could start over our friendship. However, I think he felt so ashamed that he cut all ties with us. We reached out a few times to his wife, but did not hear a response. We left well enough alone and assumed the friendship was over.

When I got back from the hospital, I received this e-mail from him. This is just a portion of what he said.

> "Later that night I got the word you were doing even worse and things were grave. I cried a lot that night, knowing I could never ask for your forgiveness or ever regain your friendship. I begged God that night for you. I begged God that night that he would spare your life.
>
> I have to be honest that a little part of my prayer was selfish. I begged God to give me a chance to make things right.
>
> I am so grateful to God that you are alive today. I am so glad for Doug and your children. I am so grateful to God that thousands upon thousands of people witnessed a

great miracle. I truly believe your miracle was for a greater purpose. It was to show that prayer is real and powerful and efficacious! I am so glad to know you will do many more great things for God's kingdom in this life. I am also grateful I have a chance to make things right and I can hopefully work towards regaining your friendship."

Honestly, I never expected to receive this letter from him. It was heartwarming and I knew he was sincere. I wrote him back and simply said, "All is forgiven. I hold no grudge. Let us just continue to keep in touch and start a new friendship."

Reading his e-mail made me think of all the people I know who are estranged from a certain family member or a friend and it makes me want to call each and every one of them and say, "It's not worth it! What if they died? You missed all that time with them!" It was clear that if I had died, he would have lived with regret, and there is nothing worth living with regret!

Heightened Innocence

What is strange about waking up after experiencing death is that my purity was heightened. It was as if I were a baby born with great innocence. It was like I did not have a mean bone in my body and my normal sarcasm was gone. If people talked poorly about someone else, I would hurt for that person. I did not even want to turn on the TV. It gave me a sick feeling and I did not want it to take away this innocence. I had this keen awareness of sin and evil. I have to be honest—I loved the feeling. It was refreshing and I wanted to hold on to it forever and let nothing disturb that state of mind and body. I had a truly joyful heart. Every wall I had ever built was gone, and it was like starting anew. If I had to use one word to describe it in earthly terms, it would be "peace." I was in a great state of peace. So when this friend asked for my forgiveness, I had no problem because any grudge from the past I may have had against him, or anyone else for that matter, was completely wiped away upon waking up from death.

Apostolic Pardon

I expressed this new sense of purity and innocence to many of my friends, wondering why dying and coming back to life would make me feel this way. It was in writing this book and uncovering so many details that I think I have the answer.

Father Parks told me that when they administered the Anointing of the Sick, Father Muir gave me the Apostolic Pardon, a plenary indulgence. This is done right before someone dies in order to free them from any punishments they might have from their sins. It saves them from spending time in purgatory, so they may go straight to heaven. The words of the prayer explain the meaning of the act:

> Through the holy mysteries of our redemption may almighty God release you from all punishments in this life and in the life to come. May he open to you the gates of paradise and welcome you to everlasting joy. …By the authority which the Apostolic See has given me, I grant you a full pardon and the remission of all your sins in the name of the Father, and of the Son, and of the Holy Spirit.

Wow! That is powerful! To think I received that pardon for the punishments of my sins makes me feel like if I had died, I would surely be in heaven. My sister, Kari, said to me after leaving the hospital, "I think the Lord erased your memory because if you had remembered seeing him or seeing heaven, you would have never come back to us, and God wanted you to come back." She was probably right! And I strongly feel the peace I woke up with was a taste of heaven. I never remembered seeing the light, but I will never forget the heavenly peace I felt after dying.

Chapter Eighteen
WHAT DOESN'T KILL YOU MAKES YOU STRONGER

*A*fter the assembly in high school when I announced my sister's name as the winner when she was not, I ran for cover. I hid in the gym until every last person left the building…and I mean every last person was gone before I showed my face. I came out from hiding and walked up to my mom and dad and said in a sulking voice, "Okay, I'm ready to go home." My mother replied, "Where do you think you are going? You still have half-a-day of school to finish."

In complete shock, I replied, "Oh, no, Mom! There is no way I am sticking around here. I am going to be the laughingstock, the butt of every joke. There is NO way I am staying at school today. We should think about me switching schools. I do not think I can return here."

My mother and father looked at me with sympathetic eyes, as if they understood my pain. To my utter horror they both said, "No, you are staying in school today because this moment is not going to define you forever. Sure, kids may tease you and make fun of you, but you need to walk down the halls and hold your head up high and ignore them." Their tone changed to one of force as they boldly went on to remind me, "You are a Welsch and we do not run and hide. We face things head on. In a few days everyone will forget. What does not kill you will make you stronger." How could they do this to me? My parents? My protectors? Here they were feeding me to the lions.

Suffering

That was one of the toughest days of my high school experience. I faced the ridicule and it was definitely a strengthening experience for me. What is crazy is that I became a speaker later in life after having the worst thing that could happen while giving a talk—the whole crowd booing. But I survived and it toughened my skin. By making me take the hard road and refusing to rescue me from that situation, my parents revealed to me that suffering was not beyond me and suffering through things would make me stronger. That day was not the first time I suffered in life and it surely was not the last.

When I woke up from critical care, I knew the road to recovery was going to be hard; but without a doubt, I knew I had the strength. "What doesn't kill me will make me stronger." I was alive, I was alive! I did not die. I was confident that when all the suffering was through, my strength would grow enormously, and it did. I had the strength to survive.

Why Me?

When I returned home, over one thousand different people had gone to my support page to receive updates about my condition. About five hundred new people asked to become my friends on Facebook, and while normally I do not accept friend requests from people I do not know, I accepted every single person, because somehow through prayer we were connected. These people were my support and community, offering up comments and prayers for me on a daily basis. It was nothing I had ever seen before.

Many were from different parts of the United States and some were from other countries. One woman in particular was from the Middle East. She told me how she prayed for me. Another woman wrote me because she had heard about another woman who had just died from an amniotic fluid embolism and she was trying to come to grips with it. She sent me the woman's blog, which the family updated regularly. It broke my heart.

She was a young mom in her thirties just like me. She had three children already when she and her twin babies died. I instantly responded by writing a comment to the family, but after reading it over, I deleted it. I wanted to share that my family and I knew what they were going through and that we could relate to their pain; but the truth is, we did not know the extremes of what they were going through because as extreme as things were for us, I lived. I erased my comments to the family because I thought they would not want to hear that I survived. Maybe I was feeling "survivors guilt" and worried it might leave them angry, asking why not my mom, wife, sister...why did she not survive, too? Instead, I simply wrote, "I am praying for you." I do not know why I survived when others do not.

Although I felt that family would not want me to share my story, another family found comfort in my survival. I spoke with a husband and wife who lost their five-year-old daughter suddenly from illness, and as I sat there not knowing how to begin comforting them in their incredible sorrow, they said to me, "Your story gives us hope. We know it was our daughter's time to go back to heaven because if it wasn't her time, God would have moved heaven and earth as he did for you to save her life." I was amazed as I listened to this couple's faithfulness.

Making Sense of My Survival and Suffering

The women in my online AFE support group and I share one amazing thing in common. Our survivals were miracles. Each person on the site describes her existence in that same manner. As I was trying to make sense of how I felt after going through this ordeal, I saw a post from another woman on the site. It said, "Being a survivor of AFE makes me feel incredibly grateful and incredibly undeserving at the same time." She could not have expressed my feelings any better. I do not know why I survived when so many do not. The answer is one I will only find when I get to heaven. For now, all I can do is live the rest of my life to the absolute fullest! Wednesday morning, July 28, 2010, I died and I physically came back to life; but emotionally, mentally, and spiritually I will never be the same. My old self died and I returned to life with a new awakening of my soul. I feel like God is calling me to reach out to those who are suffering and listen to them with compassion and pray for their healing.

Six months after my AFE, a heartbroken woman wrote me saying, "My sister died of an AFE after having her first child." She went on to say, "My niece is healthy and wonderful. However, what my sister went through haunts me." She wanted to talk to me about my experience. I was nervous to speak with her but felt like the Lord had somehow prepared me for this conversation, so I called her immediately, not knowing how I could help or what I would even say.

She asked me many questions, searching for insight into what her sister experienced. It was clear she was looking for a reason why this happened, trying to figure out if her sister and I shared any common labor experiences that led to our AFEs. I told her I have compared my situation to that of other survivors and realized there are no commonalties among any of us. I told her I beat myself up in the beginning wondering if it was the HSG test I received days before conceiving, if I was too stressed in pregnancy, if it was the epidural, or if it was how they broke my water, but all I have come up with is that it is a mystery. Women who experienced AFEs have experienced them before their labor and after, before their epidural and after, before their water breaking and after, so really there is nothing to pinpoint a cause, which is very frustrating. I feel this gave her comfort, knowing her sister could not have done anything differently to avoid having her AFE.

At one point, the woman said, "While my sister was having her emergency C-section, we were at home dancing and singing in excitement." She revealed how horrible she feels now knowing her sister was dying during that time. It was clear she was trying to blame herself and find fault in her actions, maybe as a way to cope. I said to her with certainty and in a firm tone, "You did exactly what you were supposed to be doing during that time. You were celebrating the birth and life of your niece. Your niece lived, and your sister would have wanted you to celebrate. Never regret that time!" I went on to say, "As a woman who was in your sister's shoes, I can tell you when I woke up from death to find out how much my family and friends were suffering, I did not want them to feel that way. Had I died, I would not have wanted them to be sad or be miserable. I would have wanted them to live and to be joyous so that my daughter would see a world filled with joy. Your niece needs your joy. Your sister would not want you to be in this kind of pain." She thanked me for talking and asked if the rest of her family could call me. She felt it might help their healing as well.

As I have opened up publicly to share my story, there have been many people who have revealed to me their great suffering, like the man from Italy whose wife left him after ten years, the 18-year-old who strayed from her faith, the 33-year-old woman who was shot through the heart in a robbery, the sick elderly woman, the man with four children who lost his job, and many women suffering from miscarriages and others from infertility. My eyes have been opened to the incredible amount of suffering in our world, but all of these people were not without hope. Their faith was pulling them through. It makes me wonder how people suffer without faith. Faith gives suffering purpose. Jesus suffered, and it brought about the Resurrection—new life! No one is immune from it. I wish I was an expert on the subject of suffering to help people understand it more, but I am not. I have in my own mind tried to make sense of it, and have been left even more uncertain about why or how suffering comes about, but what I am certain of is God meets us in the center of it. Christ joins our suffering to his on the cross, and God works through suffering to bring about hope and healing. God has the power to bring us from the depths of darkness, even the darkness of death, and bring us into the light!

The Attack Continues

Is the devil still throwing roadblocks at me to deter me from living life to its fullest? Absolutely! And I am sure he will as long as I continue to defend the dignity and sanctity of life and fight for God's honor. In fact, five months after the AFE incident, I was editing this book's chapter, "A Little Background." I had just finished reading the sentence

"Many times I felt attacked by the evil one, but I am constantly vigilant in knowing where my enemy is at all times," when my husband called to tell me our other house, which had just sold, and after the new buyer had completed the inspection and appraisal process, had flooded. One of the toilet tanks cracked and water had been gushing for at least two days. We were set to close on the house three weeks later, but the damages were so bad that all the tile, carpet, and wood flooring had to be removed. Hearing this news made me sad and somewhat annoyed, but not angry like it would have before the incident. Before, I would have had smoke coming out from my ears and been on fire for days. The devil may still be after me, attempting to "throw arrows" to annoy me in every way possible, but it does not make me angry because I AM ALIVE, and now more than ever, I believe in the "armor of God" and the protection of the Lord. Even if I am alive in a flooded house, I am still alive. My family is healthy, we are together, and that is all I need in life.

Where Will I Go from Here?

Now that I am alive, I want to live life louder and make my mark in this world bigger and better. I want to help end abortion and all other evils. I want to pray like a saint and live like one, too. I want to love my husband in a way that lets him know how wonderful he is every moment of his life. I want to raise my children to grow up to be saints....yes, saints! I want to be there for them so they never, NEVER question their worth or dignity. I want every member of my family to know the depths of what I feel for them. I want my friends to always feel loved and supported by me. I want to have the courage to wear my heart on my sleeve. I want to speak about the power of prayer and the wonders God can work though any and all tragedy and suffering. I want to change the world one soul at a time by reaching into the hearts of people and speaking to their greatest hunger…their hunger for the Lord. I want them to know the merciful, all knowing, all loving God—the God of Miracles—the God who heals through suffering—the God that I know. So I will speak a little louder and a whole lot prouder.

Practically, will I be able to accomplish everything on this list? Only time will tell, and time is what I have been given. Working through the hands of doctors and nurses, God chose to save my life and completely heal me for some reason. I have been given the gift of life not once, but twice. I AM ALIVE to bring glory to God, to try my hardest, to be completely present to my life, and to live my life to the fullest with no regrets! The day I died will not define me; every day I continue to live to make a difference will. When I die, I want to go to heaven, so I will continue to live a life that will get me there, and I will do my best to bring as many of you as I can with me! This is my story, and my story will live on. Praise be to God! Amen!

Endnotes

1. Ephesians 6:10–20, NAB.

2. Faddis, Chris. (2010). Urgent Prayer Request: Melanie Pritchard in Critical Condition. Retrieved November 10, 2010, from http://www.livinggracefully.net

3. Ibid.

4. Henry, Mark (2010). Pro-Life Speaker Melanie Pritchard's Miraculous Recovery. Retrieved November 13, 2010, from http://www.catholic.org

5. Ibid.